THE 100 GREATEST SONGS OF ALL TIME

First published in the UK by Sona Books, an imprint of Danann Publishing Limited

CAT NO. **SON0616**

Project editor: Martin Corteel

Book design: Darren Grice

Proof reader: Cameron Thurlow

Cover images: Getty Images

Printed in E.U.

ISBN: **978-1-915343-85-7**

THE 100 GREATEST SONGS OF ALL TIME

Carolyn McHugh

sona BOOKS

CONTENTS

INTRODUCTION

Explore 100 of the greatest songs ever recorded...

More than a collection, this book is a celebration of musical genius, cultural milestones and the timeless artistry that has shaped the soundtrack of our lives.

From pop to rock, folk, funk and soul, ballads to bangers, these songs represent the best of music since 1950s early rock and roll.

Each entry tells the story behind the song, including the creative process, cultural impact and legacy. You'll learn about the heartbreak that inspired poignant ballads, the social movements behind anthems of change and the moments that led to chart-topping hits. We honour the artists who pushed boundaries, the producers who crafted masterpieces, the songwriters whose lyrics became iconic and the performers whose voices made history.

While providing a comprehensive assessment of the absolute best in musical achievement, the selection of tracks is inherently subjective. Everyone has their own favourites and feelings about what makes a song truly great. This list is meant to spark conversation and debate, encouraging readers to reflect on their own musical journeys and the songs that have defined their lives.

A sizeable number of the entries date from the 1960s and 1970s, a period which saw an explosion of creativity and innovation, as artists experimented with new sounds, genres and recording techniques. The cultural and social upheavals of those decades provided fertile ground for musical expression, resulting in a flurry of fantastic tracks that still resonate today.

Whether you're a dedicated music fan or a casual listener, this collection aims to remind you of the songs that have shaped our world. It's a testament to music's enduring power and a tribute to the songs that will continue to inspire future generations. Start your journey through these 100 great songs, each one a timeless work of art that connects, uplifts and unites us.

DAVID GEFFEN COMPANY
NIRVANA
DGCT 5
Side A
45 rpm
stereo
SMELLS LIKE TEEN SPIRIT (LP Version)

WHAT A WONDERFUL WORLD

LOUIS ARMSTRONG

1968

100

WRITTEN BY: Bob Thiele (credited as George Douglas) and George David Weiss

RECORDED: 16 August 1967

PRODUCER: Bob Thiele

ENGINEER: Uncredited studio engineer

RELEASED: 18 October 1967

W*hat a Wonderful World* is an uplifting jazz song that captures a sense of optimism and appreciation for the simple beauty of life.

The lyrics celebrate everyday wonders, such as trees of green, red roses and the love and connection between people, almost as if seen through the eyes of a child. However there was an interesting contrast with that sense of childhood as Armstrong's famously deep, gravelly voice added real warmth and sincerity to the song, while the production included opulent orchestral arrangements.

It's claimed that the idea behind the song was to provide comfort amidst the escalating problems in America during the late 1960s, particularly around racial tensions and the ongoing Vietnam War.

However, the song was not a success in the United States initially, reportedly due to limited promotion. However, it was a huge international hit, especially in the UK where it went to #1. Then over time, the song gained immense popularity and became one of Louis Armstrong's most beloved tracks.

The song's inclusion in the 1987 film *Good Morning, Vietnam*, starring Robin Williams, played a significant role in revitalising its popularity in the late 1980s, so that when it was re-released in 1988 it made #32 on the US Billboard Hot 100.

Check out these covers ...

As symbol of hope and positivity, the song has been widely used and covered. One of the most acclaimed versions came from Eva Cassidy who gave her usual soulful and heartfelt performance.

In 2002 Tony Bennett & k.d. lang produced a duet version brings a fresh perspective to the song, on their album *Wonderful World*.

EVA CASSIDY

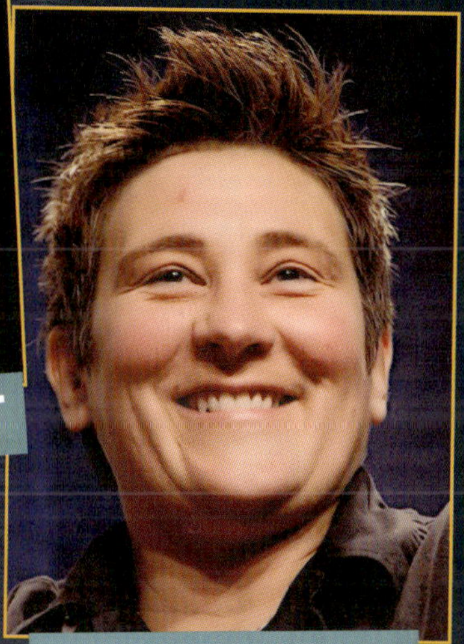

K.D. LANG

TONY BENNETT

ALL RIGHT NOW

FREE

1970

99

WRITTEN BY: Andy Fraser and Paul Rodgers

RECORDED: January 1970

PRODUCER: Free (with uncredited assistance from John Kelly)

ENGINEER: Roy Thomas Baker

RELEASED: 15 May 1970

Free's lead singer Paul Rodgers and bassist Andy Fraser reportedly wrote *All Right Now* in about 10 minutes after a concert at Durham University where they felt their setlist had lacked a strong, uplifting final song to energize the crowd and leave them wanting more.

It was included as the final track on the band's third and breakthrough album *Fire and Water*, where it ran to 5:33 with an extended guitar solo and outro. When the band's record label issued it as the second pre-released single from the album, which the band were initially loath to do, it was cut to 4:14 and became a huge hit – making #4 in America and #2 in the UK.

Catapulting the bluesy rock band to international fame, the song has gone on to sell millions of copies worldwide and is among the elite group of songs to achieve multi-million US radio plays. The song's popularity also helped the band score an appearance at the great 1970 Isle of Wight Festival where they played to an audience of 600,000 people – the largest musical event ever at that time, beating 1969's Woodstock in America.

For such an impactful and enduring song it has a pretty straightforward, feel-good story about a man trying to impress a woman and persuade her to spend time with him. Yet it perfectly captures the spontaneity and excitement of youthful attraction – and has powerful structure and a memorable guitar riff by the band's celebrated guitarist Paul Kossoff.

Check out these covers ...

Rod Stewart was an enthusiastic fan of the song in the 1970s and became known for performing it live, although he didn't have a hit single with it. Free's renowned lead vocalist Paul Rodgers continued to perform the song live, including during his time with Queen.

The 1980 version by Mike Oldfield of *Tubular Bells* fame is worth a listen. Then, in 1991, a remix by producer Bob Clearmountain reached #8 on the UK chart.

ROD STEWART

MIKE OLDFIELD

DANCING QUEEN
ABBA
1976

98

WRITTEN BY: Benny Andersson, Björn Ulvaeus and Stig Anderson

RECORDED: Between August 1975 and March 1976

PRODUCER: Benny Andersson and Björn Ulvaeus

ENGINEER: Michael B. Tretow

RELEASED: 16 August 1976

From ABBA's fourth studio album, 1976's *Arrival*, *Dancing Queen* is a celebration of joy and dance which has become one of the super group's most popular tracks.

The disco-influenced track is characterised by its upbeat tempo, catchy melody and grand orchestration. It opens with a distinctive piano swirl, followed by a rhythmic beat, rich harmonies and Agnetha Fältskog and Anni-Frid Lyngstad's soaring vocals, celebrating the joy and freedom of dancing, while young and carefree. The idea was to emulate the sound and feel of dance music, drawing inspiration from songs like George McCrae's *Rock Your Baby* and the overall vibe of disco music at that time.

The song received widespread acclaim from critics and remains a staple on lists of the greatest pop songs of all time, praised for its production quality, vocal performance and emotional resonance.

As one of ABBA's best-selling singles, it spent a week at #1 in the US and six weeks at #1 in the UK, as well as topping the charts in several other countries. It wasn't written about the Swedish royal family, but its first live performance holds a royal connection as ABBA performed the song live for the first time on 18 June 1976, at a televised gala in honour of Swedish King Carl Gustaf XVI's marriage to Silvia Sommerlath.

Check out these covers ...

Dancing Queen has been featured in various films, TV shows and musicals, including the hit musical and film *Mamma Mia!*. Cher covered *Dancing Queen* for her ABBA tribute album of the same name, bringing a fresh perspective to the classic while preserving its joyous spirit.

MAMMA MIA! MUSICAL

CHER

JOLENE
DOLLY PARTON

1973

97

WRITTEN BY: Dolly Parton

RECORDED: 22 May 1973

PRODUCER: Bob Ferguson

ENGINEER: Al Pachucki

RELEASED: 15 October 1973

This famous country song tells the story of a woman confronting a beautiful, seductive woman named Jolene, whom she fears might steal her man. The song is noted for its narrative style, with vivid imagery and a melancholic melody that captures the desperation and vulnerability of the singer.

The arrangement is relatively simple, featuring a prominent and distinctive acoustic guitar riff which is among the most recognisable elements of the production, complemented by subtle bass and restrained percussion that allow Parton's vocals to shine. It also features a minor key which further contributes to the haunting and pleading tone.

Dolly Parton has explained that the inspiration for the song came when a redheaded bank clerk flirted with her husband, Carl Dean. She chose the name Jolene when she heard it later from a young fan who asked for an autograph and felt it was a good fit.

That interaction with a bank clerk certainly added to Parton's financial well-being after the song reached #1 on the Billboard Hot Country Songs chart, and #7 in the UK, making it one of Parton's most successful singles overseas, as well as enjoying further success internationally.

Check out these covers ...

The White Stripes produced one of the most famous covers of *Jolene* back in 2000 when they added a raw, rock-infused production. Jack White's impassioned vocal delivery and the band's stripped-down instrumentation brought a whole new intensity to the song.

Miley Cyrus has frequently performed *Jolene*, including a well-received acoustic version as part of her 2012 'Backyard Sessions'. Her cover pays homage to her godmother, Dolly Parton, while introducing the song to a younger audience.

Most recently Beyoncé gave the song a bold new twist on her 2024 country-inspired album, *Cowboy Carter*.

In her reimagined version, she replaces Parton's pleading with a fierce warning that Jolene needs to stay away from her husband and family. This fresh take adds a powerful and modern edge to the beloved country anthem.

THE WHITE STRIPES

BEYONCÉ

SWEET DREAMS (ARE MADE OF THIS)

EURYTHMICS

1983

96

WRITTEN BY: Annie Lennox and Dave Stewart

RECORDED: Late 1982

PRODUCER: Annie Lennox and Dave Stewart

ENGINEER: Adam Williams

RELEASED: 21 January 1983 (UK) and May 1983 (US)

This was the song that gave the Eurythmics their breakthrough. It was their biggest ever hit in the US, where got to #1 on the Billboard Hot 100, and it also topped the charts in France and Canada and made #2 in the UK.

Featuring a minimalist arrangement with emphasis on the electronic soundscapes typical of the early 1980s new wave genre it is an important synthpop track which has gone on to become the Eurythmic's signature song.

Lennox and Stewart had got together as a duo following the disbandment of their previous outfit The Tourists and *Sweet Dreams* was reportedly written in the unhappy aftermath of the break-up.

The song was born out of improvisation and experimentation,

The Tourists

including the distinctive synth riff – from the Roland SH-101 synthesizer – that became the track's backbone. The bassline and synthesizer parts were developed spontaneously, with Lennox and Stewart layering their ideas until the track took shape.

'The song was an expression of how I felt: hopeless and nihilistic,' Lennox has said. However, Dave Stewart added the 'hold your head up, moving on' refrain to make the lyrics more uplifting.

Fun fact

The song's music video, which featured striking visuals, including Lennox's androgynous appearance and the use of surreal imagery, such as cows in a boardroom, became one of the most popular ever on MTV.

Check out these covers ...

One of the most famous covers came from Marilyn Manson in 1995, whose version transformed the song into a dark, industrial metal anthem. This cover reached #26 on the Billboard Hot 100.

MARILYN MANSON

COMMON PEOPLE

PULP

1995

95

WRITTEN BY: Jarvis Cocker, Nick Banks, Steve Mackey, Russell Senior, Candida Doyle and Mark Webber

RECORDED: June 1994

PRODUCER: Chris Thomas

ENGINEER: David Nicholas

RELEASED: 22 May 1995

This standout song of the Britpop era fair bristles with incisive lyrics about the British class system, all driven along by an insistent throbbing beat.

As a commentary on class tourism it is hard to beat as it highlights the divide between the working class and those who romanticise their lifestyle without understanding the hardships.

It's funny – but singer Jarvis Cocker is heard simmering with irony and frustration as he delivers the lyrics with increasingly energetic fervour.

The song tells the story of a wealthy girl who wants to live like 'common people' and the narrator's frustration with her naive romanticisation of poverty. Jarvis Cocker has said that the lyrics were inspired by a Greek art student he once met while studying at Central Saint Martins College of Art and Design in London. Theories abound as to who the woman might be, but Cocker can't remember.

It was the lead single from the fifth studio album, *Different Class* by alternative rock band Pulp. While it was more of a cult hit in the US, in the UK it was a major success in the UK where it peaked at #2.

The song has also been used in various political contexts to comment on class issues, including by left-wing political groups and campaigns.

Fun fact

Cocker says that he wrote the riff that was the basis of the song on a Casio keyboard.

Check out these covers ...

One of the most famous covers is by actor William Shatner of *Star Trek* fame and featured on his 2004 album *Has Been*. Produced by Ben Folds, Shatner's version transforms the song into a spoken-word piece with dramatic intensity – adding contempt where Cocker was indignant. Folds, who produced Shatner's version, has also performed the song live, adding his own unique piano-driven style to it.

WILLIAM SHATNER

BEN FOLDS

WHEN A MAN LOVES A WOMAN

PERCY SLEDGE

1966

94

WRITTEN BY: Calvin Lewis and Andrew Wright

RECORDED: 17 February 1966

PRODUCER: Quin Ivy

ENGINEER: Marlin Greene

RELEASED: 16 April 1966

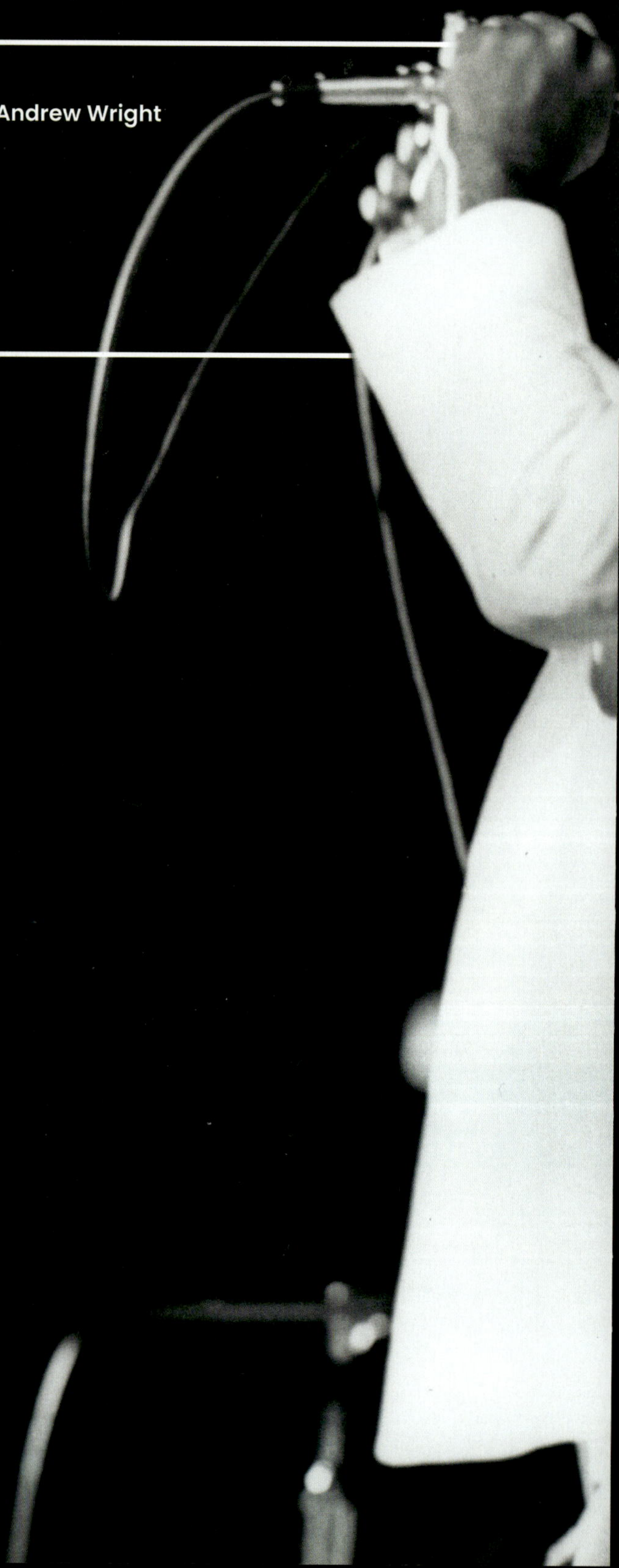

Percy Sledge's impassioned and heartfelt vocal delivery is the standout feature of *When a Man Loves a Woman*, helping to make it one of the greatest love songs of all time.

The song's lyrics create a vivid portrayal of the lengths one goes to for love, expressing unwavering devotion, even to the point of sacrifice.

This recording features a slow, bluesy arrangement with prominent organ and brass sections. It was Percy Sledge's debut single – and remains his most famous song.

Although he doesn't have a writing credit on the track, Sledge has claimed that he should have received an acknowledgement as the song was based on his personal experience of a broken relationship which he had shared with the team. Certainly his raw and emotional vocal performance reverberates with the profound feelings of a man deeply in love and was recorded in just two unbeatable takes.

Becoming a million-seller, it made #1 in the US on the Billboard Hot 100 and R&B Charts and got to #4 in the UK at the time. It returned to the British charts in 1987, peaking at #2, after it was featured in a TV advert for Levi Jeans.

Check out these covers ...

Bette Midler covered the song in 1979 for the soundtrack of the film 'The Rose' which was loosely based on the life of singer Janis Joplin. Bringing her own powerful vocal interpretation to the classic, Midler released her track as a single the following year and got to #35 on the Billboard Hot 100.

But Michael Bolton had the biggest success when he covered the track on his seventh studio album, *Time, Love and Tenderness*, in 1991. His version reached #1 in the charts and won him a Grammy for Best Male Pop Vocal Performance.

BETTE MIDLER

MICHAEL BOLTON

Fun fact

Bolton's cover is also notable for being the final #1 number-one song to chart on the Billboard Hot 100 chart based on sales and airplay reported by phone and messenger services before switching over to the Nielsen SoundScan system, which integrated more accurate point of sale information.

FAIRYTALE OF NEW YORK
THE POGUES (FT. KIRSTY MACCOLL)

1984

93

WRITTEN BY: Shane MacGowan and Jem Finer of The Pogues

RECORDED: 1987

PRODUCER: Steve Lillywhite

ENGINEER: Steve Lillywhite

RELEASED: 23 November 1987

To hone a list of 100 great songs there have to be 'rules' – and one of them, for this book, was no Christmas songs – but there had to be an exception for this 'anti-Christmas' tale blending elements of punk and folk and enlivened and elevated by the vocals of the late lamented British singer Kirsty MacColl.

Fairytale of New York tells the story of an Irish immigrant's Christmas Eve reverie about holidays past, while sleeping off a drinking session in a New York City drunk tank. The song features a duet between Pogues' front man Shane MacGowan and guest vocalist Kirsty MacColl, with a narrative that juxtaposes nostalgia and bitterness, romance and realism.

Apparently writers Shane MacGowan and Jem Finer conceived *Fairytale of New York* in 1986, as a duet featuring MacGowan and Pogues' then bass player Cait O'Riordan, having taken the title from J.P. Donleavy's novel of the same name. However, they missed the window to release it as a Christmas single and by the time they got into the studio to record the song in 1987, O'Riordan had left the band. Steve Lillywhite, who was producing The Pogues, suggested that his wife Kirsty MacColl record a scratch vocal. Her performance was so impressive that the band kept it, foregoing the idea of bringing in a more famous singer such as Chrissie Hynde.

Peaking at #2 in the UK when it was first released in 1987 – kept off the much coveted Christmas #1 spot by The Pet Shop Boys' cover of the Elvis classic *Always On My Mind* – it has since been re-released several times and, due to the arrival of streaming services, has reached the UK Top 20 on twenty separate occasions, including every year since Christmas 2005.

In December 2023, following the death of Shane MacGowan on 30 November, the song went to #1 in Ireland and #4 in the UK and was certified sextuple platinum in the UK. While it is the 'most-played' Christmas song of the 21st century and the fifth 'most charted' song of all time in the UK, it is too British and idiosyncratic ever to have troubled the American charts.

Check out these covers ...

Irish folk singer Christy Moore recorded a notable cover of the song, adding his own emotional depth to the rendition, then Ronan Keating & Maire Brennan produced a well-received version in 2000, which brought the song to a broader pop audience.

Ed Sheeran performed a version of the song with Anne-Marie for BBC Radio 1's Live Lounge in 2017, which was praised for its contemporary take on the classic.

CHRISTY MOORE

RONAN KEATING

MAIRE BRENNAN

SWEET CAROLINE
NEIL DIAMOND
1969

92

WRITTEN BY: Neil Diamond

RECORDED: 1969

PRODUCER: Tom Catalano

ENGINEER: Brooks Arthur

RELEASED: 28 May 1969

S*weet Caroline* is a timeless classic that has captured listeners' hearts to become a cultural staple and a sporting anthem.

Over the years Neil Diamond has said the song was written for several different people including his wife, his childhood sweetheart and most famously US President John F. Kennedy's daughter Caroline.

When first released it peaked at #8 in the UK charts, and #4 in the US, where it gained Platinum status. Since then it has gone on to become a crowd favourite at sports events and other public gatherings, thanks largely to its 'bom, bom, bom' and 'so good' refrains.

Characterised by its catchy melody, sing-along chorus and uplifting mood, the soft rock song features a prominent brass section, a memorable piano intro and Neil Diamond's signature vocal style.

The song's adoption by the Boston Red Sox baseball team first turned it into an unofficial sports anthem in the late 1990s. It got picked up at other sports venues and public gatherings around the world, before gaining a new lease of life in 2021 during the

2020 UEFA European Football Championship (Euro 2020), which took place in 2021 due to the COVID-19 pandemic. The song became the anthem for the England national football team, with fans singing it passionately during and after matches. Its popularity soared following England's successful run to the final, as its feel-good vibe resonated with fans.

Check out these covers ...

While Elvis never recorded a studio version of *Sweet Caroline*, his live renditions have been captured on several live albums and concert recordings, including the live album *On Stage: February 1970*. The Elvis version stands out for its lively and energetic interpretation, characteristic of his Las Vegas performances in the early 1970s.

Another of the 'greats', Frank Sinatra, frequently performed the song live, without recording it, adding his unique style and interpretation.

ELVIS

FRANK SINATRA

MACARTHUR PARK
RICHARD HARRIS

1968

91

WRITTEN BY: Jimmy Webb

RECORDED: Late 1967/early 1968

PRODUCER: Jimmy Webb and Armin Steiner

ENGINEER: Armin Steiner

RELEASED: 22 April 1968

Including some of the most inexplicable lyrical metaphors in all of pop history – linking love with cake baking and melting green icing – this huge and bonkers song was an unexpected hit for its unexpected singer, the actor Richard Harris.

At seven minutes and 21 seconds long, the song is a sprawling, surreal and ambitious piece, blending elements of pop, rock and orchestral music. It is divided into distinct sections each with its own mood and tempo changes, culminating in an emotive and dramatic finale.

Lyrically, the song tells a surrealistic tale of love and loss in MacArthur Park, a real park located in Los Angeles. The lyrics are known for their vivid imagery and unconventional narrative structure, while the references to cake left out in the rain is to symbolise the ephemeral nature of love and memories.

Richard Harris, known primarily as a theatre actor, was chosen to sing *MacArthur Park* due to his friendship and previous collaboration with songwriter Jimmy Webb, who envisioned *MacArthur Park* as a complex and theatrical song, requiring a dramatic interpretation. He believed that Richard Harris's theatrical background and deep, emotive voice would be ideal for conveying the song's intricate lyrics and emotional depth.

Harris, who had a passion for music and had dabbled in singing before, saw recording the song as an opportunity to explore his musical talents further.

Certainly his theatrical delivery and powerful vocals added a distinctive flavour to the song, contributing to its memorable and impactful rendition. It gave him a hit single, reaching #2 on the Billboard Hot 100 chart in the US and #4 on the UK Singles Chart and selling over one million copies globally.

Check out these covers ...

While Richard Harris's original version is iconic, Donna Summer's 1978 disco rendition is widely regarded as the best cover. Her version not only topped the charts but also introduced MacArthur Park to a new generation as she transformed the song into a disco masterpiece. With its intricate arrangement and extended instrumental breaks, which became a hallmark of disco music, Donna Summer's track, with her powerful vocals, went to #1 in the States and #5 in the UK.

DONNA SUMMER

Fun fact

Although the song is titled McArthur Park – and that was what the song's writer Jimmy Webb sang when he recorded the track himself in 1996 – when the song was a hit for Richard Harris and Donna Summer they sang about 'MacArthur's Park'.

LIKE A PRAYER
MADONNA
1989

90

WRITTEN BY: Madonna and Patrick Leonard

RECORDED: September 1988

PRODUCER: Madonna and Patrick Leonard

ENGINEER: Bill Bottrell, Michael Hutchinson and Patrick Leonard

RELEASED: 3 March 1989

Recognising that her fans were growing up, and keen for them not to pack her away with their teenage things, Madonna was looking for something different and danceable when she wrote *Like a Prayer*, about her relationship with God. The result was a powerful and controversial hit song combining pop, rock, gospel and funk elements – even a gospel choir to add a layer of drama and soul.

As Madonna explored a complex relationship with her Catholic religion roots and personal empowerment, she came up with double entendre lyrics which blended religious imagery with personal reflection and a sexual undertone. The overall sound is both spiritual and secular.

The song was groundbreaking and marked a significant turning point in Madonna's career, showing her willingness to tackle controversial themes. The song's release was accompanied by a music video which featured provocative religious imagery, including scenes of Madonna dancing in front of burning crosses and receiving stigmata. This sparked widespread debate and controversy, particularly with religious groups, but also earned praise for its bold artistic vision.

Like a Prayer was part of Madonna's fourth studio album of the same name. It was a commercial juggernaut, reaching #1 on the US Billboard Hot 100, where it remained for three consecutive weeks. It also topped the UK Singles Chart, marking Madonna's sixth #1 single in the UK and becoming one of the best-selling singles of the year. While the single was a worldwide hit, also making #1 in Canada, Australia, Italy, Ireland and Sweden, the album itself was also huge, selling over 15 million copies globally.

Its chart-topping performance, significant sales and profound impact on pop culture and music make it a standout track in Madonna's illustrious career.

Check out these covers ...

The song is often credited with helping to redefine the boundaries of pop music and has been covered and referenced by numerous artists. Rita Ora, Miley Cyrus and Kelly Clarkson have all performed it live, while it's been recorded by artists as diverse as the cast of TV show *Glee*, and French electronic music group, Mad'House.

MILEY CYRUS

RITA ORA

KELLY CLARKSON

glee

Fun fact

Before the song's official release, Madonna signed a deal allowing Pepsi to use *Like a Prayer* in a commercial. After the music video release was deemed controversial, Pepsi pulled the ad but allowed Madonna to keep her $5 million endorsement fee.

RUN
SNOW PATROL
2003

89

WRITTEN BY: All members of Snow Patrol

RECORDED: 2003

PRODUCER: Jacknife Lee

ENGINEER: Jacknife Lee

RELEASED: 26 February 2004

Characterised by its sweeping sound, driving rhythm and hopeful 'Light Up' chant, the anthemic song *Run* was a breakthrough hit for Snow Patrol, helping to establish them as a major force in alternative rock.

It begins with a gentle, melancholic guitar riff that gradually builds into a powerful crescendo. The song's raw lyrics, touching on themes of love, support and perseverance, are delivered with real emotional intensity by lead singer Gary Lightbody.

Beautifully crafted, its sad theme of farewell to a lover is leavened by the repeated 'Light Up' line, suggesting better times ahead. This is particularly powerful during live performances and the track is always a concert highlight.

It peaked at #5 on the UK Singles Chart and #15 on the US Billboard Modern Rock Tracks. As a key track on the band's album *Final Straw* it also strongly contributed to that album's success, which included gaining multi-platinum status in the UK and gold certification in the US.

Check out these covers ...

Leona Lewis's cover of *Run* stands out as the most commercially successful and critically acclaimed reinterpretation of the song. The arrangement in Lewis's version is more orchestral and grander than the original, featuring strings and a more pronounced build-up, which enhances the song's anthemic quality. This version gave Lewis her third UK #1.

Other significant covers have come from classical cross-over singer Katherine Jenkins, and Josh Groban known for his classical pop-fusion, have helped to keep *Run* relevant.

LEONA LEWIS

KATHERINE JENKINS

JOSH GROBAN

AGAINST ALL ODDS
PHIL COLLINS

1984

88

WRITTEN BY: Phil Collins

RECORDED: 1983

PRODUCER: Arif Mardin

ENGINEER: Phil Collins and Hugh Padgham

RELEASED: 25 February 1984

***Against All Odds* is a powerful break up song, characterised by its emotional intensity. It features a heartfelt vocal performance by Collins, with its soaring melody accompanied by lush orchestration and a prominent piano line.**

Phil Collins was the drummer and then lead singer for the hugely influential and successful rock band Genesis and had originally written a song, which would become *Against All Odds,* during sessions for the Genesis album *Duke*. He wrote from his personal experience of going through a divorce at the time and eventually decided that the subject matter was too personal for a group song and instead decided to save the song for a planned solo album.

He was then approached to contribute a song to the soundtrack of the film *Against All Odds* and reworked and re-titled his song for that. His track has since gone on to overshadow the film, reaching #1 on the US Billboard Hot 100 and #2 on the UK Singles Chart. It was also Grammy nominated for Best Pop Vocal Performance and Golden Globe and Oscar nominated as Best Original Song composed for a film.

Check out these covers ...

The most commercially successful cover came from Mariah Carey in 1999, in a version featuring the Irish boy band Westlife. It charted in several countries and made #1 in Canada.

MARIAH CAREY

WESTLIFE

Fun fact

Phil Collins performed *Against All Odds* at both Live Aid concerts in London and Philadelphia on 13 July 1985, famously using the supersonic airliner Concorde to travel between the two cities and make rock history.

YOU'VE GOT A FRIEND
CAROLE KING
1971

87

WRITTEN BY: Carole King
RECORDED: January 1971
PRODUCER: Lou Adler
ENGINEER: Hank Cicalo
RELEASED: 10 February 1971

This song was popularised by two artists at more or less the same time. As the originator of this beautiful ballad, the credit here goes to Carole King, but the cover by her friend and frequent collaborator James Taylor was actually more commercially successful. Carole King nudges the acknowledgment here because the song was at the heart of her phenomenally successful, Grammy award-winning album *Tapestry* – a commercial juggernaut which was #1 on the Billboard 200 album chart for 15 consecutive weeks and remained on the chart for nearly six years.

Focusing on unwavering support and friendship, Carole King's soothing piano accompaniment and rich vocals are complemented by simple yet profound lyrics, creating an intimate and comforting atmosphere. The arrangement is soft and soulful, featuring subtle orchestration and backing vocals that enhance its emotional depth. The story goes that she wrote it as a reply 'you've got a friend right here' to James Taylor's lyric in his 1970 hit *Fire and Rain* claiming he could not find a friend. The song won the Grammy Award for Best Pop Vocal Performance, Female, for Carole King and Grammy Award for Best Male Pop Vocal Performance for James Taylor in 1972. This unique achievement underscores the song's universal appeal and the exceptional interpretations by both artists.

James Taylor

Check out these covers ...

James Taylor's cover, which was released in April 1971, became more commercially successful, charting at #1 in the US and at #4 in the UK. Carole King and James Taylor often performed the song together, and both versions are equally cherished. The Taylor version is also on his album *Mud Slide Slim and the Blue Horizon.*

Dusty Springfield also recorded the song, performing a soulful version which was released in the UK. But the next act to have a hit with their cover was the English pop band McFly who released the song along with their original track *All About You* as a double A-side official charity single for the 2005 Comic Relief appeal. This got to #1 in the UK and Ireland and is in fact the band's best-selling single.

OLIVER'S ARMY

ELVIS COSTELLO AND THE ATTRACTIONS

1979

86

WRITTEN BY: Elvis Costello

RECORDED: 1978

PRODUCER: Nick Lowe

ENGINEER: Roger Bechirian

RELEASED: 2 February 1979

From his 1979 album *Armed Forces*, the song *Oliver's Army* is singer-songwriter Elvis Costello's most widely acclaimed and commercially successful single – also his highest-charting, clocking up three weeks at #2 in the UK.

It features a pop-rock style with new wave influences. The catchy melody is highlighted by the prominent use of piano, which was played by Steve Nieve, a member of The Attractions.

Inspired by Costello's visit to Belfast in 1978, it's a protest song with lyrics addressing political and social issues, particularly focusing on the British military presence in Northern Ireland at the time and criticising the use of young soldiers in such conflicts. The song's lyrics are a critique of military recruitment practices, particularly how

the young men sent to fight are often from economically deprived areas.

The title references Oliver Cromwell, who ruled England in the mid-1600s after the civil war.

With its catchy melody and ABBA-esque piano riff opening, the song is often cited as a classic example of Costello's ability to blend pop sensibilities with serious lyrical content.

Check out these covers ...

No single cover stands out as the definitive version, as the original remains the most celebrated.

But one notable cover is by the English band Blur. Give it a listen and see if you agree with Damon Albarn's view that it was 'one of the worst things' the band ever recorded.

DAMON ALBARN OF BLUR

WITHOUT YOU
NILSSON
1971

85

WRITTEN BY: Pete Ham and Tom Evans of Badfinger

RECORDED: 1971

PRODUCER: Richard Perry

ENGINEER: Phil Brown and Richard Perry

RELEASED: October 1971

Harry Nilsson produced what became the definitive version of this poignant ballad with his emotive vocal performance, which ranges from a tender, almost whispering quality in the verses to a powerful, soaring delivery in the chorus.

The dramatic impact of the song is further driven by the sumptuous orchestration, including piano, strings and layered harmonies, which add to its dramatic impact.

The song was originally written and recorded by the British rock band Badfinger for their 1970 album *No Dice*, although it didn't achieve the same level of acclaim or commercial success. Initially, band members Pete Ham and Tom Evans had written parts of separate songs, then during a recording session, Evans played his 'I can't live ...' chorus for Ham, who realised it could perfectly complement his verses. The combination resulted in the emotionally powerful but straightforwardly rock structure of their original *Without You*.

The story goes that Nilsson heard the Badfinger track at a party and thought it sounded like a Beatles number. He believed he could bring something to the song and recorded it for his album *Nilsson Schmilsson*, reportedly breaking down in tears as he sang in the studio, perfectly capturing the agony of lost love.

Released as a single, the track reached #1 in the US and the UK, among other charts, for four and five weeks respectively, and won Nilsson the Grammy Award for Best Male Pop Vocal Performance at the 1973 ceremony.

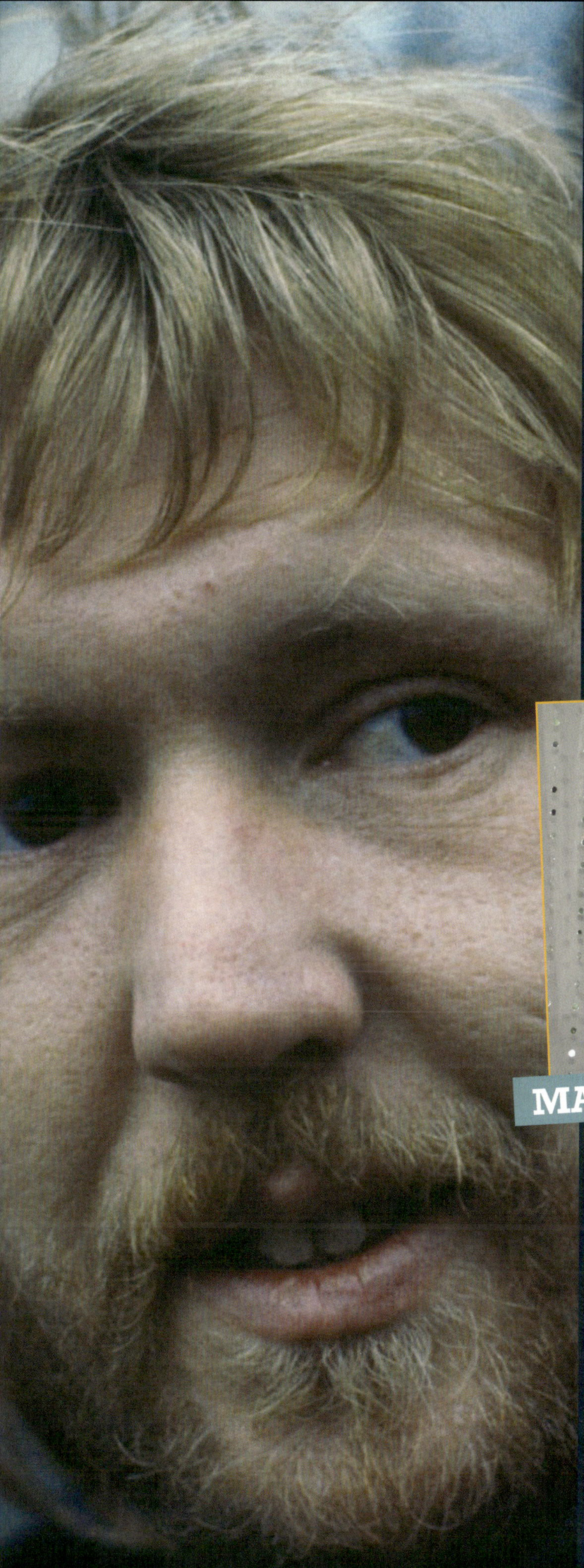

Check out these covers …

Mariah Carey's version was a considerable success – coincidentally released in the US in January 1994, just days after Nilsson died which gave it an extra resonance. It topped the charts in multiple countries, including the UK, where it was #1 for four weeks.

Other versions of this much-covered track have come from Australian soft rock group Air Supply, Shirley Bassey, Heart and Clay Aiken.

And of course, although not a cover – it's interesting to give the Badfinger original a spin too.

MARIAH CAREY

HEART

BADFINGER

GET IT ON
T. REX
1971

84

WRITTEN BY: Marc Bolan
RECORDED: Early 1971
PRODUCER: Tony Visconti
ENGINEER: Roy Thomas Baker
RELEASED: 24 July 1971 (UK) Early 1972 (US)

This is one of the defining tracks of glam rock – a music movement which stormed the UK in the early '70s, with Marc Bolan and his band T Rex among its leading architects.

From their album *Electric Warrior,* which was hugely successful, *Get It On* was the band's biggest commercial hit and most critically acclaimed single, reaching #1 on the UK Singles Chart, where it remained for four weeks. It also gave Bolan his biggest hit stateside when it made #10 on the Billboard chart, (retitled as *Bang a Gong (Get It On)* to avoid confusion with another track by the group Chase).

With its blend of glam rock and boogie, *Get It On* epitomises Glam Rock's fusion of rock and roll with flamboyant, theatrical style and catchy, rhythmic melodies. The song features a prominent, driving guitar riff, boogie-woogie piano and sultry saxophone, combined with Marc Bolan's distinctive, laid-back vocal delivery. The lyrics are playful and suggestive, contributing to the song's allure and appeal.

Check out these covers ...

Rock supergroup The Power Station, which included Robert Palmer, Andy Taylor, John Taylor (both from Duran Duran) and Tony Thompson (ex-Chic) released their version as a single in 1985 and reached #9 in the US and #22 in the UK.

Blondie included a live version for their hit album *Parallel Lines* in 1979 and Frankie Goes to Hollywood have also covered this track.

THE POWER STATION

BLONDIE

LOVE AND AFFECTION
JOAN ARMATRADING
1976

83

WRITTEN BY: Joan Armatrading

RECORDED: 1976

PRODUCER: Glyn Johns

ENGINEER: Glyn Johns

RELEASED: September 1976

***Love and Affection* is a timeless piece that beautifully showcases Joan Armatrading's talent as a songwriter and vocalist. From her self-titled debut album, it reached # 10 on the UK Singles Chart, to give Armatrading her first major hit.**

Blending elements of folk, rock and blues, the song opens with a gentle acoustic 12-string guitar riff, supported by a subtle yet effective arrangement of strings and horns. Armatrading's powerful and emotive vocal delivery, capturing the feelings of vulnerability and yearning is at the forefront.

The song has influenced a wide range of artists and is often cited as a pioneering work in the singer-songwriter genre, as it blends introspective lyrics with a rich musical arrangement. The extensive experience and expertise of the track's producer Glyn Johns, who had worked with The Rolling Stones, The Who and Led Zeppelin, hugely contributed to the polished yet heartfelt sound of the recording.

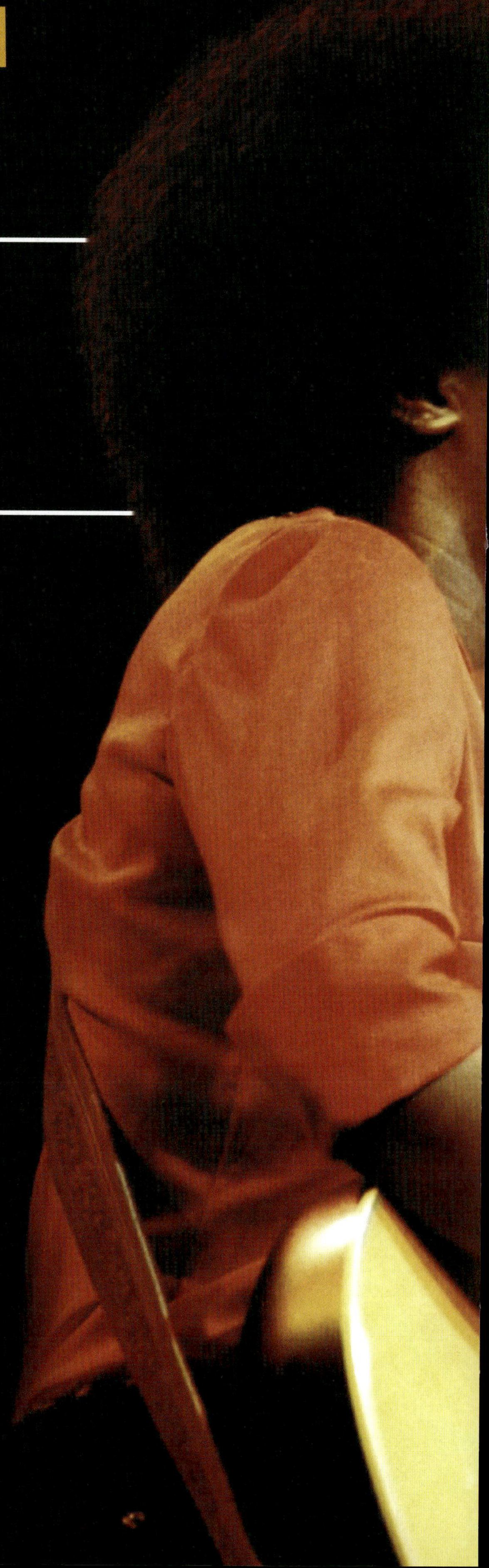

Check out these covers ...

It's been covered aplenty. Sheena Easton sang it for her 1984 platinum album *A Private Heaven*. Sinitta charted at #62 in the UK in 1990 with a disco-flavoured version, while Courtney Pine and Kele Le Roc produced a jazz version.

Armatrading has said that her favourite version is the one by Texan band Two Nice Girls in 1989 when they used it in a medley with Velvet Underground's *Sweet Jane*, called *Sweet Jane with Affection*.

SINITTA

SHEENA EASTON

TWO NICE GIRLS

COURTNEY PINE

THE SCIENTIST
COLDPLAY
2002

82

WRITTEN BY: Chris Martin, Jonny Buckland, Guy Berryman and Will Champion

RECORDED: Over 2001–2002

PRODUCER: Ken Nelson and Coldplay

ENGINEER: Ken Nelson

RELEASED: 4 November 2002

This poignant, piano-driven ballad showcases Coldplay's signature sound of emotive melody with heartfelt lyrics. It features Chris Martin's plaintive vocals, layered with a simple yet powerful piano riff, lush strings and understated guitar work. The song's lyrics deal

with themes of regret and apology sung by a lover seeking reconciliation and wishing to turn back time.

Almost stately in its grandeur, the song played a huge part in solidifying Coldplay's reputation as one of the leading bands of the early 2000s, as they marched on to amass countless awards including nine Brits and seven Grammys. *The Scientist* made #10 in the UK, and while it didn't perform as strongly on the mainstream charts in the US, reaching #18 on the Billboard Modern Rock Tracks chart, it received significant airplay and supported the incredible success of the album it came from – *A Rush of Blood to the Head*, which sold over 15 million copies worldwide.

Undoubtedly a modern classic, Chris Martin has said that the song came together quickly after he found an old piano in the studio and began playing the chord progression that became the basis for *The Scientist*.

Check out these covers ...

Several female singers have changed the angle when covering it, including Natasha Bedingfield, Corinne Bailey Rae and Avril Lavigne. Aimee Mann's 2003 version, featured on her live album *Lost in Space*, adds a distinct folk-rock flavour to the song.

Willie Nelson brought a country twist to the song with his cover in 2011.

AVRIL LAVIGNE

NATASHA BEDINGFIELD

CORINNE BAILEY RAE

PARANOID ANDROID
RADIOHEAD
1997

81

WRITTEN BY: Thom Yorke, Jonny Greenwood, Ed O'Brien, Colin Greenwood and Phil Selway

RECORDED: Between September 1996 and March 1997

PRODUCER: Nigel Godrich and Radiohead

ENGINEER: Nigel Godrich and Radiohead

RELEASED: 26 May 1997

This ambitious and grand lead single from Radiohead's revered album *OK Computer* distilled the inspiring elements that made the band so admired, while teetering almost on the edge of a prog rock energy which was new for them.

A richly layered song that captures the anxieties and complexities of modern life, exploring themes of alienation, technological dystopia and societal decay, it was reportedly inspired by the experiences of the band's lead singer Thom Yorke, during a violent and chaotic night out in Los Angeles.

Its intricate composition was influenced by, and a tribute to, two other monster songs, *Bohemian Rhapsody* by Queen and *Happiness is a Warm Gun* by The Beatles. Like those tracks, the song is a multi-part epic, (six and a half minutes long) experimental and quite brilliant. Its four distinct sections, varying in tempo and mood, begin with a melancholic acoustic guitar and Thom Yorke's ethereal vocals, which give way to cryptic lyrics before transcending into a heavier rock segment with distorted guitars and aggressive vocals. The third section features a slow, mesmerising passage with choir-like harmonies and a surreal atmosphere. Finally, the song concludes with an intense guitar solo and a return to the earlier themes, ending on a powerful and climactic note.

Fun fact

The 'Paranoid Android' of the title is a reference to Marvin the Paranoid Android from Douglas Adams' science fiction series *The Hitchhiker's Guide to the Galaxy* – a robot who suffers from depression and paranoia, symbolising the song's themes of mental distress and existential angst.

Check out these covers ...

Like its forebears, *Bohemian Rhapsody* and *Happiness is a Warm Gun*, the song is a tough one to cover. One of the best reinterpretations came from Australian singer-songwriter Sia who performed a haunting and stripped-down cover of *Paranoid Android* highlighting the song's emotional depth.

Reggae collective Easy Star All-Stars included a cover on their reggae/dub tribute album *Radiodread* reinterpreting the song in a completely different musical style.

SIA

EASY STAR ALL-STARS

STAYIN' ALIVE
BEE GEES
1977

80

WRITTEN BY: Barry Gibb, Robin Gibb and Maurice Gibb
RECORDED: 1977
PRODUCER: The Bee Gees, Albhy Galuten and Karl Richardson
ENGINEER: Karl Richardson
RELEASED: 13 December 1977

This disco anthem captured the spirit of the late 1970s – with its catchy melody, danceable beat and themes of resilience and survival ensuring its place in music history.

An upbeat disco song, characterised by its driving bass line, falsetto vocals and infectious rhythm, it features a distinctive guitar riff, a prominent horn section and layered harmonies that became signature elements of the Bee Gees' sound.

The lyrics, conveying themes of resilience, survival and confidence, reflect the band's observation of the character and vitality of people in New York City, encapsulating the spirit of the disco era.

The song's association with the hit film *Saturday Night Fever*, and leading man John Travolta's iconic dance moves, has solidified its place in popular culture. The *Saturday Night Fever* soundtrack became one of the best-selling albums of all time, with *Stayin' Alive* as one of its standout tracks, helping the Bee Gees reach new heights of fame and commercial success.

The song sold millions around the world, reaching #1 on the Billboard Hot 100, where it stayed for four consecutive weeks, and peaking at #4 in the UK.

Fun fact

The song's tempo of 103 beats per minute makes it a recommended track for performing CPR, as it aligns closely with the ideal rate of chest compressions.

Check out these covers ...

The British electronic music group N-Trance released a dance version of *Stayin' Alive* in 1995 which became a hit in its own right, reaching # 2 in the UK.

TUTTI FRUTTI
LITTLE RICHARD

1955

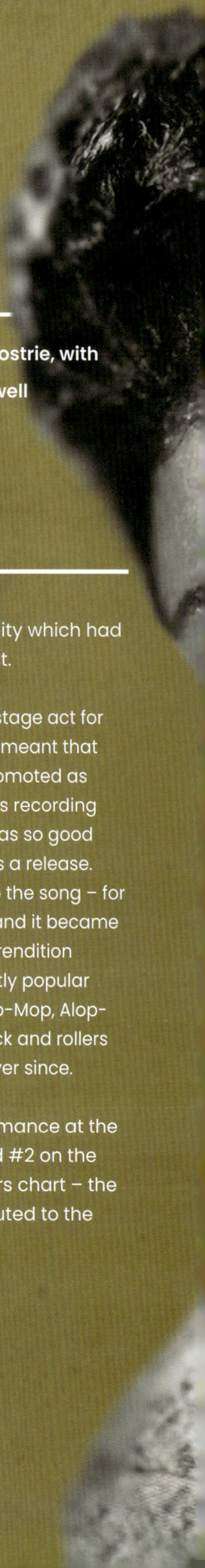

79

WRITTEN BY: Little Richard (Richard Penniman) and Dorothy LaBostrie, with contributions from producer Robert 'Bumps' Blackwell

RECORDED: September 1955

PRODUCER: Robert 'Bumps' Blackwell

ENGINEER: Cosimo Matassa

RELEASED: November 1955

The influence exerted by this Little Richard track is simply staggering. Credited as being the 'architect of rock and roll' and described by an admiring Elvis as 'the greatest', Little Richard created the new 'rules' of rock and roll – number one of which was, 'Be Loud!' *Tutti Frutti* was his first big hit – a fiery and unique sound, incorporating suggestive lyrics with a unique singing style. Its energetic performance, bold lyrics, combined with Little Richard's energetic performance and exuberant delivery, set a new standard for rock music, while the song's rhythm was the basis for what became the standard beat of rock music.

Tutti Frutti gave Richard his first R&B hit in the USA and launched him into an unsuspecting world. This screaming and showy singer/songwriter/pianist extraordinaire, was wilder and raunchier than anyone before him. He was a genuine original – a mixed race, bisexual performer, slightly built, with mascara on his lashes and pompadour hair piled upon his head – with flare and femininity which had never been seen before in a male artist.

Although the song had been part of his stage act for some time, the sexual nature of its lyrics meant that it would never have been released or promoted as a single. However, during one of Richard's recording sessions, it was decided that the song was so good that, with sanitised lyrics, it could work as a release. Songwriter Dorothy LaBostrie cleaned up the song – for example substituting 'booty' for rooti' – and it became a major hit. Richard's upbeat, energetic rendition of somewhat gibberish lyrics was instantly popular and his opening cry of 'Awop-Bop-a-Loo-Mop, Alop-Bam-Boom' became a clarion call to rock and rollers everywhere which has kept its appeal ever since.

Despite relatively modest chart performance at the time – #17 on the Billboard Hot 100 and #2 on the Billboard Rhythm and Blues Best-Sellers chart – the song's success internationally contributed to the global spread of rock and roll music.

Check out these covers ...

Tutti Frutti had a profound impact on artists like Elvis Presley, The Beatles and many others who have cited Little Richard as a major influence. Elvis recorded the song for inclusion on his first album, while The Beatles regularly sang it live between 1960 and 1962, although no recorded version is known. In differing style, '50s crooner Pat Boone made #12 with his version in 1956.

Queen played the song during their 1986 Magic Tour and so it appears on their album *Live at Wembley Stadium*.

THE BEATLES

PAT BOONE

QUEEN

LIGHT MY FIRE
THE DOORS

1966

78

WRITTEN BY: Robby Krieger
RECORDED: August 1966
PRODUCER: Paul A. Rothchild
ENGINEER: Bruce Botnick
RELEASED: 24 April 1967

Blending rock, psychedelic and jazz influences, *Light My Fire* is one of The Doors' most famous and influential songs.

It played a significant role in establishing the band's reputation and was a cornerstone of the 1960s counterculture movement.

Light My Fire features a signature extended instrumental break with Ray Manzarek's intricate keyboard work and Robby Krieger's flamenco-inspired guitar playing. Jim Morrison's deep and expressive vocals add to the song's seductive feel.

It also helped propel The Doors' self-titled debut album, released in January 1967, to commercial success and critical acclaim. The original album version of *Light My Fire* is over seven minutes long, featuring an extensive keyboard and guitar solo. For the single release, the song was edited down to about three minutes to make it more radio friendly. Although primarily written by Robby Krieger, the guitarist of The Doors, other band members including Jim Morrison, Ray Manzarek and John Densmore made significant contributions.

Check out these covers ...

This is a much-covered track. One of the most famous, which turned the song into a slower, Latin-influenced acoustic ballad, came from acclaimed Puerto Rican guitarist José Feliciano in 1968. This version became a hit in its own right, reaching #3 on the Billboard Hot 100.

In 1970 Shirley Bassey brought a powerful and dramatic interpretation to the song and then Amii Stewart did well with her 1979 disco-style cover, which reached #5 on the UK Singles Chart.

Pop Idol contest winner Will Young shepherded the song into the new millennium with his pop-oriented rendition which was #1 in the UK for two weeks in 2002.

JOSÉ FELICIANO

SHIRLEY BASSEY

Fun fact

When The Doors famously performed *Light My Fire* on The Ed Sullivan Show in 1967, Sullivan asked the band to change the lyric 'girl, we couldn't get much higher', because of its drug reference. The band agreed but then performed the original lyrics live, leading to a ban from future appearances on the show.

HANDBAGS AND GLADRAGS

STEREOPHONICS

2001

77

WRITTEN BY: Mike d'Abo

RECORDED: 2001

PRODUCER: Steve Bush and Marshall Bird

ENGINEER: Steve Bush and Marshall Bird

RELEASED: 3 December 2001

This is a poignant song that reflects on the superficiality of materialism and the importance of genuine happiness. The lyrics tell the story of an older person advising a young girl not to be seduced by the fleeting allure of fancy clothes (the gladrags) and fashionable accessories (the handbags), and the material aspects of life, as you need much more than that in life.

Yet the song's writer, Mike d'Abo, lead singer with the 1960s group Manfred Mann, was only 22 when he wrote it back in 1967.

The song's appeal undoubtedly lies in this universal and timeless message. A much-covered track, the unique interpretations brought to it by different artists over the years kept it alive.

Yet the biggest boost to its popularity came when the 2001 version by Welsh rock group Stereophonics became the theme tune for hit TV comedy *The Office*, primarily because of its melancholic yet reflective tone, which complemented the show's themes and atmosphere.

The story goes that the band recorded had only recorded their version 'as a laugh' while jamming, but their label saw its potential and decided to release it.

Stereophonics' contemporary alternative rock arrangement resonated with early 2000s audiences and at last gave the song the commercial success and chart impact it deserved as it gained its highest chart position of #4 in the UK. It was also included on the re-release of the band's album *Just Enough Education to Perform.*

Check out these covers ...

The song has been covered by numerous artists since singer Chris Farlowe first recorded it back in 1967. His soulful version didn't chart at the time but set the tone for the song's future success, not least by bringing it to the attention of Rod Stewart who was keen to record it for his 1969 debut solo album *An Old Raincoat Won't Ever Let You Down* (also known as *The Rod Stewart Album* in the US).

Rod's version is said to be writer Mike d'Abo's favourite as he was closely involved with its arrangement and production. But again it did not achieve significant chart success.

ROD STEWART

CHRIS FARLOWE

TAINTED LOVE
SOFT CELL
1981

76

WRITTEN BY: Ed Cobb

RECORDED: Mid-1981

PRODUCER: Mike Thorne

ENGINEER: Paul Hardiman and Eric Radcliffe

RELEASED: July 1981 (UK) and January 1982 (US)

Soft Cell's version of *Tainted Love* is a synth-pop cover famed for its minimalist arrangement and hypnotic rhythm. The song features a distinctive synthesizer riff and a simple, yet catchy, melody. Singer Marc Almond's plaintive and emotive vocal delivery adds to the song's melancholic yet danceable feel.

It had a significant impact on the music scene in the 1980s, becoming a defining song of the synth-pop genre and helping to popularise electronic music in mainstream pop.

Soft Cell also issued an extended 12-inch single that featured a segue into a cover of The Supremes' *Where Did Our Love Go*, which ran at over eight and a half minutes. Edited down to a more radio-friendly two and a half minutes, the song spent two weeks at #1 on the UK Singles Chart and peaked at # 8 on the US Billboard Hot 100 and spent a then-record 43 weeks on the chart.

Check out these covers ...

The original *Tainted Love* as sung by Gloria Jones in 1964 remains a classic and beloved track in the Northern Soul community. This version is upbeat soul style and directly inspired Soft Cell's interpretation which became the bigger hit.

In 2001 Marilyn Manson released another of the most famous covers, featuring a darker and heavier industrial rock interpretation. This version appeared on the soundtrack for the film *Not Another Teen Movie* and became a hit in its own right.

Then in 2005 the Pussycat Dolls cover added a pop and R&B twist to the song.

GLORIA JONES

MARILYN MANSON

PUSSYCAT DOLLS

REHAB
AMY WINEHOUSE
2006

75

WRITTEN BY: Amy Winehouse

RECORDED: 2006

PRODUCER: Mark Ronson

ENGINEER: Team including Gabriel Roth, Tom Elmhirst and Vaughan Merrick

RELEASED: 23 October 2006

The lead single from her second – and last – studio album *Back to Black*, the song *Rehab* stands as a testament to Amy Winehouse's exceptional talent and her ability to transform personal turmoil into compelling music.

Its blend of candid, autobiographical lyrics, compelling rhythm, retro-soul sound and distinctive vocals, made the song a huge critical and commercial success, becoming Amy Winehouse's signature song and ensuring its place as a classic of modern music. The lyrics also reference US singers 'Ray' (as in Ray Charles) and 'Mr Hathaway', (Donny Hathaway) who were influences on her work.

Combining a catchy melody with poignant lyrics, including the now famous 'no, no, no' refrain, the song's unflinching honesty about addiction and resistance to societal expectations struck a chord with global audiences and played a crucial part in Amy Winehouse's international breakthrough. It hit music charts throughout Europe, reaching #7 in the UK and #9 in the US, giving the young singer her first Top 10 hit stateside.

Rehab went on to win three Grammy Awards in 2008: Record of the Year, Song of the Year and Best Female Pop Vocal Performance. Winehouse also won Best New Artist and Best Pop Vocal Album for the *Back to Black* album at the same ceremony.

Despite her talents as a singer-songwriter of rare depth, Amy Winehouse battled drug and alcohol addiction, as well as mental health issues, during her short but impactful career. The song was inspired after her management team tried to persuade her to attend an alcohol rehab centre.

Rehab is also important for influencing a wave of artists in the neo-soul and contemporary R&B genres – its candid approach to personal issues and blend of retro and modern styles setting a precedent for future musicians.

It has re-entered the British charts several times, latterly in July 2011, following Amy's death, aged just 27, from alcohol poisoning.

Check out these covers ...

It's evidently hard to improve on the original in a studio, but *Rehab* has been re-interpreted live by several well-known artists including Kanye West, Justin Timberlake and Fergie.

KANYE WEST

JUSTIN TIMBERLAKE

FERGIE

(SITTIN' ON) THE DOCK OF THE BAY

OTIS REDDING

1968

74

WRITTEN BY: Otis Redding and Steve Cropper

RECORDED: 22 November and 7 December 1967

PRODUCER: Steve Cropper

ENGINEER: Ron Capone

RELEASED: 8 January 1968

Released shortly after Otis Redding's tragic death, aged 26, in a plane crash on 10 December 1967, *(Sittin' on) The Dock of the Bay* has the sad honour of being the first posthumous #1 on both the US Billboard Hot 100 and R&B charts. It was Otis Redding's only chart-topping single. His album was also the first posthumous #1 album.

The song is considered a seminal work in the soul canon and has had a profound influence across music of all genres. It stands out for its melancholic tone, poignant lyrics and Redding's moving delivery and distinctive voice, which conveyed a sense of longing and introspection.

Redding was reportedly inspired to write the song, which was something different from his usual, more romantic style, by The Beatles album *Sgt. Pepper's Lonely Hearts Club Band.*

The whistling at the end of the track, performed by Redding, is one of its most memorable features, yet is there by accident. Initially there as a placeholder until Redding came up with additional lyrics, the song's producer, Steve Cropper, decided to keep it in the final recording.

At the 11th Grammy awards, recognising the music of 1968, the song won Otis Redding the awards for Best R&B Song and Best R&B Performance.

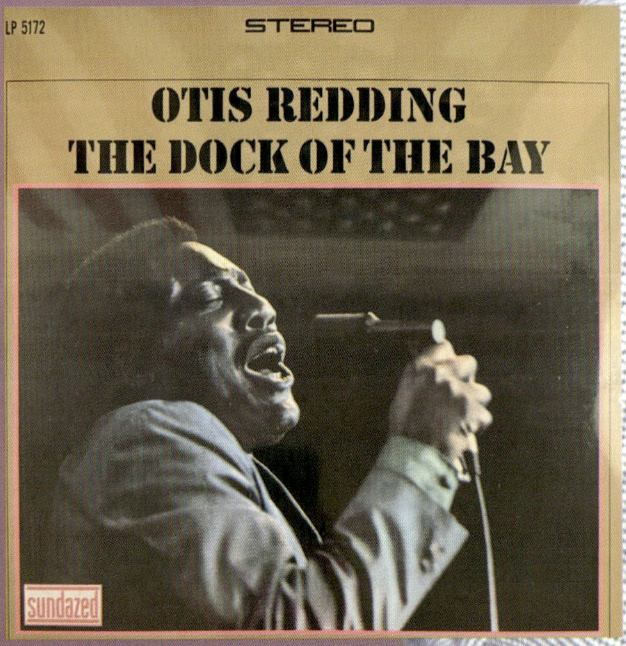

Check out these covers ...

The song has been covered by numerous artists across different genres, including rock, pop and soul. Artists such as Michael Bolton, American rock band Pearl Jam and singer/actress Sara Bareilles have all given their own renditions of the song.

PEARL JAM

SARA BAREILLES

MICHAEL BOLTON

WALK ON BY
DIONNE WARWICK
1964

73

WRITTEN BY: Burt Bacharach and Hal David

RECORDED: 1963

PRODUCER: Burt Bacharach

ENGINEER: Ed Smith

RELEASED: 26 April 1964

This cool and classy number, detailing a woman's perspective on a failed love affair, is a standout song from 1964 when it was a major hit for Dionne Warwick.

Songwriting legends Hal David (lyrics) and Burt Bacharach (music) wrote it especially for her as she emerged as a star vocalist in her own right after years as a session singer.

It was initially used as the B-side to her single *Any Old Time of The Day* – viewed by her record label as a 'last chance' at making the charts. But the decision by influential DJ 'Murray the K's' to play *Walk On By* in preference to the A-side actually made the song a hit, reaching #6 on the Billboard chart and blasting Warwick to transatlantic success.

The collaboration between Bacharach and David was one of the best partnerships in history. Writing hundreds of songs together, they created a sophisticated sound that became synonymous with 1960s soul and placed Dionne among the greatest singers of the decade. The three worked together many times resulted in other classics including *I'll Never Fall in Love Again* and *Wishin' and Hopin'*.

Warwick's vocal delivery was praised for its elegance and emotional restraint as her phrasing and intonation brought out the nuances in the lyrics and melody.

Bacharach's arrangement, with full orchestration including strings, brass and woodwinds, add to the song's impact. Its unexpected chord changes and progressions were a hallmark of Bacharach's award-winning style.

Check out these covers ...

This song has been covered many, many times – check out Isaac Hayes' whopping 12 minute take on his 1969 album *Hot Buttered Soul* and the version by punk band The Stranglers on their album *Black and White* in 1978.

ISAAC HAYES

THE STRANGLERS

Burt Bacharach, Dionne Warwick, and Hal David 1996

I'M A BELIEVER
THE MONKEES
1966

72

WRITTEN BY: Neil Diamond
RECORDED: 15 October 1966
PRODUCER: Jeff Barry
ENGINEER: Hank Cicalo
RELEASED: 12 November 1966

I'm a Believer **was a huge hit for The Monkees, a manufactured band created for a TV show. The song was prominently featured in the series, helping boost its popularity and propel it to massive commercial success.**

A classic of the 1960s pop-rock era, the song is about the transformative power of love. The narrator, initially sceptical about finding true love, becomes a believer after experiencing it firsthand. The upbeat and catchy lyrics, combined with a memorable melody, proved perfect in encapsulating the joyful realisation of falling in love.

It was one of the fastest selling singles of all time, certified Gold within two days of its release, peaking at #1 on the US Billboard Hot 100 where it stayed for seven weeks, and also topping the UK chart. It helped solidify Neil Diamond's reputation as a talented songwriter when it went on to sell over 10 million copies worldwide.

Micky Dolenz, the Monkees' drummer and vocalist, performed the lead vocals on the track.

Check out these covers ...

The original songwriter, Neil Diamond, has performed his own version of the song, while The Four Tops gave a soulful rendition in 1967.

Comedians Vic Reeves and Bob Mortimer teamed up with The Wonder Stuff for a rather surreal version in 1995 which reached #3 on the UK Singles Chart.

Then a whole new generation came to love the song when Smash Mouth covered it for the soundtrack of the 2001 film *Shrek*. Another comedian, Eddie Murphy, performed a version of the song as the character Donkey in the *Shrek* movies.

NEIL DIAMOND

THE WONDER STUFF

SMASH MOUTH

I SAY A LITTLE PRAYER
ARETHA FRANKLIN

1968

71

WRITTEN BY: Bert Bacharach and Hal David

RECORDED: April 1968

PRODUCER: Jerry Wexler

ENGINEER: Tom Dowd and Arif Mardin

RELEASED: July 1968

A hit for two black American female singers, Dionne Warwick and Aretha Franklin, it's one of only a few pop songs to take the listener through the domestic details of life (putting make up on and going to work) while navigating life and love.

Dionne Warwick had the first – and million-selling – hit with it in in 1967, stressing the spiritual element of the lyrics and reaching #4 in the US charts.

But then, just a year later, the song came to be owned by Aretha Franklin, who included her gospel-driven version on her album *Aretha Now*, making it stronger, adding swank and sass and injecting a sense of urgency to her voice which gave the song a new meaning and a second life in the charts. It reached #10 on the Billboard Hot 100 chart and #3 on the Hot R&B/Hip-Hop songs chart and #4 on the UK Singles Chart giving Aretha her biggest UK hit.

The Sweet Inspirations provided the distinctive backup vocals on Aretha's recording, adding to the song's rich, layered sound.

Written while the Vietnam War was raging, the song resonated with many listeners experiencing separation and uncertainty, including those affected by the war who took it as a message of support for the American soldiers out there.

Dionne Warwick

Check out these covers ...

Jamaican singer Diana King covered *I Say a Little Prayer* in 1997 for the soundtrack of the film *My Best Friend's Wedding*. Her reggae-infused version brought a fresh, upbeat take to the song. Annie Lennox often performed a cover of the song during her live performances, the British electronic music group Bomb the Bass released a cover in 1988, which reached #10 on the UK Singles Chart.

ANNIE LENNOX

BOMB THE BASS

THE FIRST CUT IS THE DEEPEST

ROD STEWART

1976

70

WRITTEN BY: Cat Stevens

RECORDED: 1976

PRODUCER: Tom Dowd

ENGINEER: Andy Johns and Tom Dowd

RELEASED: November 1976

Released as a single from his hit album *A Night on the Town*, Rod Stewart's version of this multi-covered song reached #1 in the UK and #21 on the Billboard Hot 100 in 1977 and remains one of his most enduring songs.

By the time Rod released his cover of the song, which became the biggest hit version, it had already been covered by several other artists. But as a leading figure in 1970s rock music, able to transform a song with his distinctive voice and style, Rod's rendition has proved to be definitive and brought the song to a broader audience, solidifying its status as a classic.

There are however many fans of writer Cat Stevens's original recording, for his album *New Masters*, released in December 1967. While his version was not a major hit, it laid the groundwork for subsequent covers and is still praised for its sentimental essence, incorporating elements of folk and rock, characteristic of his early work as a singer-songwriter.

But it was Rod Stewart's emotionally intense delivery which proved perfect at getting across the song's exploration of recovering from a broken heart. Combined with a powerful production arrangement, which brought a distinctive depth to the song's melancholic yet hopeful message, the lyrics reflect the deep emotional scars left by a first love, and the challenge of opening up to love again.

The song's success contributed to the phenomenal performance of Rod Stewart's seventh album *A Night on the Town* which was certified multi-platinum in various countries and reached #1 in the UK and #2 in America.

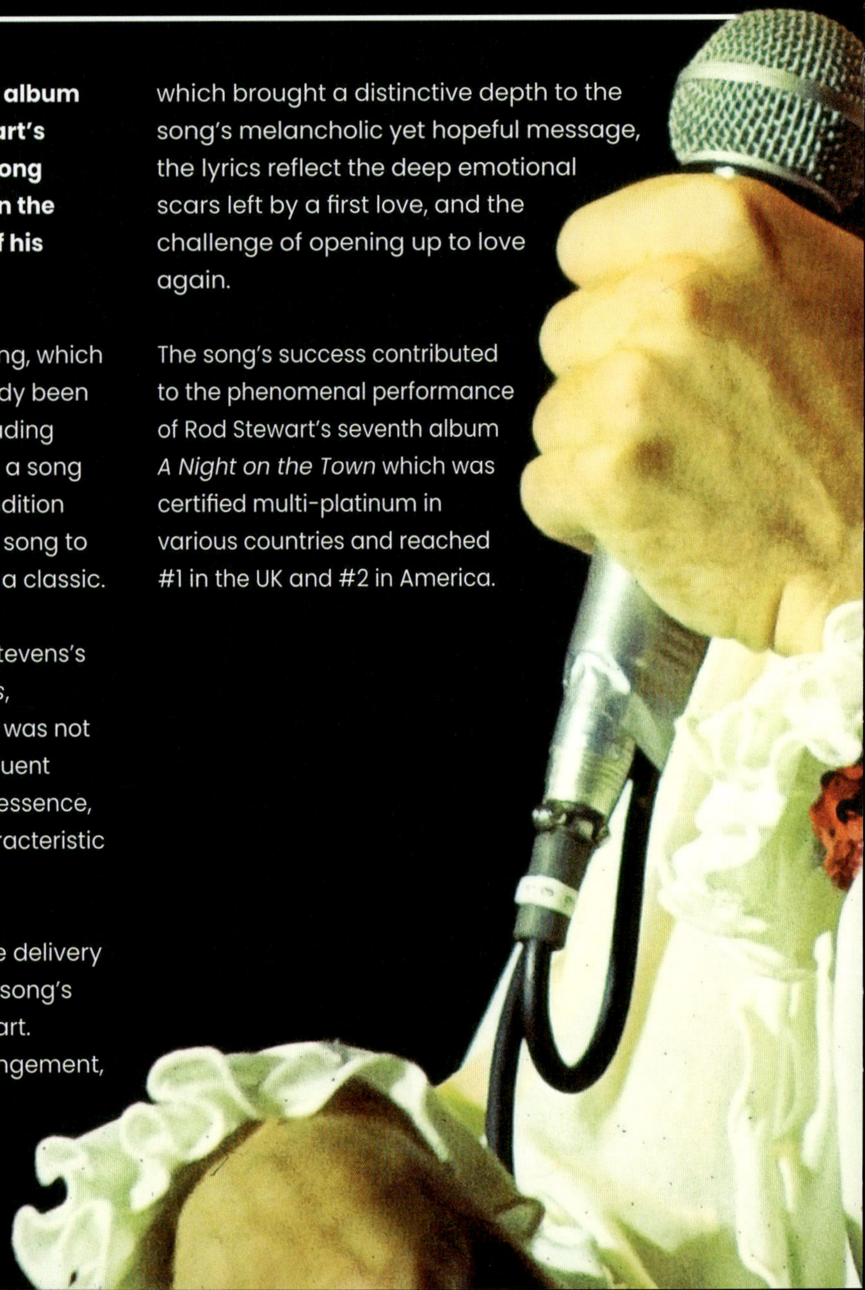

Check out these covers ...

The First Cut is the Deepest has been covered many times – a testament to its timeless appeal and the emotional power of its lyrics and melody.

The first successful cover was by P.P. Arnold in 1967, making her debut as a singer after years as a backing vocalist for artists including Ike and Tina Turner. Her soulful rendition reached #18 on the UK Singles Chart. In that same year Jamaican singer Norma Fraser recorded a reggae version that remains popular in those circles today.

Then Sheryl Crow had an international hit with her take on the song in 2003, which reached # 14 on the Billboard Hot 100 and #1 on the Adult Contemporary chart.

P.P. ARNOLD

SHERYL CROW

YOU'VE LOST THAT LOVIN' FEELIN'

THE RIGHTEOUS BROTHERS

1964

69

WRITTEN BY: Barry Mann, Cynthia Weil and Phil Spector

RECORDED: 26 September 1964

PRODUCER: Phil Spector

ENGINEER: Larry Levine

RELEASED: November 1964

Y*ou've Lost That Lovin' Feelin'* by The Righteous Brothers is one of the most famous songs from the 1960s, with many critics describing it as one of the best recordings ever made.

All about the fading of a romantic relationship, the lyrics brilliantly convey the sense of longing and heartbreak as one partner notices the other becoming emotionally distant.

The Righteous Brothers' powerful vocal delivery underscored the emotional weight of those words, while the dramatic arrangement by Phil Spector was simply phenomenal and is regularly cited as one of the greatest examples of the 'Wall of Sound' production technique he had developed. This new production style involved layering multiple instruments and vocals to create a dense, echo-filled sound which became a hallmark of 1960s pop music.

From their album of the same name, the song proved to be the breakthrough hit for The Righteous Brothers, comprising Bill Medley and Bobby Hatfield, an American musical duo renowned for their soulful vocal harmonies. Despite their name, they were not brothers but had a close bond and voices which blended to produce distinctive harmonies which propelled them to lasting fame.

The song topped the Billboard Hot 100 chart for two weeks in February 1965 and reached #1 in the UK. It has sold millions of copies worldwide as one of the best-selling singles of all time.

At nearly four minutes long, the song was unusually lengthy for its time, so to ensure radio play, the time on the single was listed as 3:05.

Check out these covers ...

The song has continued to be a hit for the artists who have covered it since, including:

- Dionne Warwick, who released her hit version in 1969, which became a hit, reaching # 16 on the Billboard Hot 100.
- Hall & Oates who released their cover in 1980 and reached #12 on the Billboard Hot 100.
- Roberta Flack & Donny Hathaway's duet version in 1971 made #30 on the Billboard R&B chart.
- Cilla Black, whose cover version reached # 2 on the UK Singles Chart in 1965.
- Long John Baldry released a cover in 1979, which became a minor hit.
- Barry Manilow included a cover of the song on his 1989 album *Barry Manilow*.
- Neil Diamond covered the song as a duet with Dolly Parton on his 1993 album *Up on the Roof: Songs from the Brill Building*.
- Elvis Presley frequently performed the song live during his concert tours in the 1970s.

HALL & OATES

LONG JOHN BALDRY

CILLA BLACK

ROMEO AND JULIET
DIRE STRAITS

1980

68

WRITTEN BY: Mark Knopfler

RECORDED: 1980

PRODUCER: Jimmy Iovine and Mark Knopfler

ENGINEER: Shelly Yakus

RELEASED: 1981

From the 1980 album *Making Movies*, the compelling track *Romeo and Juliet* was released as a single in 1981, reputedly inspired by writer and Dire Straits lead singer Mark Knopfler's romance with girlfriend of the time, punk singer Holly Vincent, the story is about a couple breaking up because of fame.

The song has been widely praised as a modern take on the original Romeo and Juliet Shakespearean tragedy, skilfully weaving a tale of love and heartbreak with 'wry and literate' lyrics.

The vocals, instruments, composition, brilliant melody and story showcase the very best of Dire Straits, a British rock band who are among the best-selling of all time with sales of over 100 million.

Mark Knopfler's guitar solo in the song is particularly memorable and perfectly displays his distinctive fingerpicking style. Despite its failure to break into the American charts, it made #8 in the UK and is critically acclaimed as one of Dire Straits' standout tracks and a high point in their discography.

Check out these covers ...

Brandon Flowers is a huge fan of the song and his band The Killers recorded the track as the B-side on *For Reasons Unknown* and for their compilation album *Sawdust*. British folk singer-songwriter Steve Knightley included his version on his 2007 album *Cruel River*. **237**

THE KILLERS

STEVE KNIGHTLEY

EVERY BREATH YOU TAKE

THE POLICE

1983

67

WRITTEN BY: Sting

RECORDED: 1982

PRODUCER: The Police and Hugh Padgham

ENGINEER: Hugh Padgham

RELEASED: May 1983

Eighties British rock band The Police had a string of huge hits on both sides of the Atlantic during their seven-year career, but *Every Breath You Take* unquestionably stands out as their crowning achievement. Despite being commonly misunderstood as a love ballad – and even being used at weddings – the song actually delves into the unsettling psyche of a deluded stalker who confuses obsession for love.

Its creation was marred by internal strife within the band at the time as they neared their break-up, even including reported physical altercations in the studio. Sting himself, the band's lead vocalist and bassist who wrote the song when he was suffering what he described as a 'breakdown' after his first marriage ended, described it as 'a nasty little song, really rather evil'.

Released as the lead single from The Police's fifth, final and blockbusting album, *Synchronicity*, the sinister song was the band's biggest hit, selling 8 million copies in the US alone as it dominated the US Billboard Charts for eight consecutive weeks and clinched Song of the Year at the 1984 Grammy Awards. It was also #1 in the UK and many other worldwide markets, becoming one of the best-selling songs of the year.

Most radio analysis judges *Every Breath You Take* to be the most-played radio song of all time – with more than 15 million spins.

As well as Sting's nuanced vocals, the song is memorable for guitarist Andy Summers's skilful and hypnotic guitar riff which throbs away over drummer Stewart Copeland's simple but insistent beat.

Despite its enduring popularity, remember this is not a love song; it portrays something far darker and more complex.

Check out these covers ...

Sean Combs – also known as P. Diddy and Puff Daddy – famously sampled *Every Breath You Take* in his 1997 song *I'll Be Missing You*, dedicated to The Notorious B.I.G.

SEAN COMBS

LEAN ON ME

BILL WITHERS

1972

66

WRITTEN BY: Bill Withers

RECORDED: 1972

PRODUCER: Booker T. Jones

ENGINEER: Bill Halverson

RELEASED: April 1972

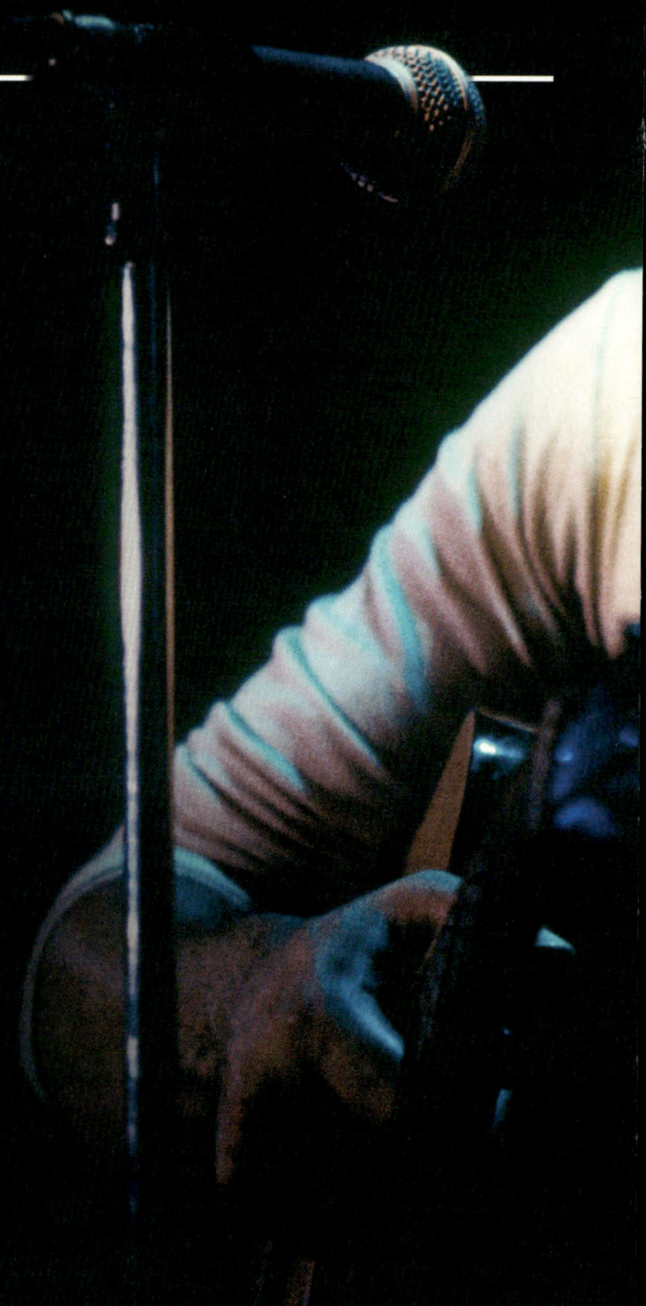

A heartfelt ballad with a simple, soulful melody and poignant lyrics about friendship and support, *Lean on Me* was the first single from Withers' second album, *Still Bill.*

Making #1 on both the American soul and Billboard Hot 100 charts, it has endured ever since as a powerful anthem of friendship and solidarity.

Withers reportedly based the song on his own experiences growing up in a poor West Virginia coal-mining town, where community support and reliance on neighbours were integral to daily life. These childhood memories came to him after he had moved to Los Angeles to pursue what became a phenomenal career as a Grammy award winning singer-songwriter, crafting thoughtful lyrics where every word counted.

Having written the song as a simple tale of rural life, Withers had no thought that *Lean on Me* would go on to become beloved as an enduring hymn-like piece which would go on to be played on big occasions as a call for union amid adversity.

Check out these covers ...

Lean on Me is among the most covered songs of the 1970s.

British glam rock band Mud covered the track in 1976, crooning away to reach #7, for what turned out to be their last appearance in the UK charts.

One of the most successful covers came later however, in 1987 when American R&B group Club Nouveau's version topped the Hot 100.

Artists Al Jarreau and Michael Bolton both successfully covered the song in the 1990s.

Mary J. Blige performed the song during celebrations to commemorate the inauguration of US President Barack Obama in 2009.

MUD

MARY J. BLIGE

AL JARREAU

MY GIRL
THE TEMPTATIONS

1964

65

WRITTEN BY: Smokey Robinson and Ronald White

RECORDED: 25 September 1964

PRODUCER: Smokey Robinson and Ronald White

ENGINEER: Norman Smith (for the recording session at Hitsville U.S.A.)

RELEASED: 21 December 1964

This masterpiece of the Motown era is universally acclaimed for its musical craft, emotional resonance and lasting impact on the music industry.

Songwriting giant Smokey Robinson co-wrote it specifically for The Temptations, instead of his own group The Miracles, to highlight the talents of The Temptations' new singer David Ruffin.

The song was a massive hit, giving The Temptations their first US #1, and became their signature number, with Ruffin's emotive and powerful delivery becoming a focal point of praise as they brought a new dimension to The Temptations' sound.

Smokey Robinson's polished production work on *My Girl* is also notable for its clean, crisp sound. The song's arrangement, including the classic bassline by James Jamerson and the melodic guitar lines by Robert White, both of the Motown session musicians known as The Funk Brothers, is also key in giving the song its sophistication and appeal.

A sweet tale of love, reflecting the optimism and romanticism of the era of its release, it's become a cultural touchstone.

Check out these covers ...

Otis Redding included a soulful rendition of the song in 1965 on his album *Otis Blue: Otis Redding Sings Soul.*

The Rolling Stones covered the song in 1967 on their *Flowers* compilation and other major artists to cover it include Al Green, The Mamas & the Papas and a young Michael Jackson who sang it in 1972 when he was aged 14.

THE MAMAS & THE PAPAS

OTIS REDDING

THE ROLLING STONES

Fun fact

The Temptations also recorded versions in German (*Mein Girl*) and Italian (*Solamente Lei*).

CRYING
ROY ORBISON
1961

64

WRITTEN BY: Roy Orbison and Joe Melson
RECORDED: July 1961
PRODUCER: Fred Foster
ENGINEER: Bill Porter
RELEASED: July 1961

This heartfelt ballad about the lingering pain of lost love is one of Roy Orbison's most celebrated songs, showcasing his powerful vocal range and emotive delivery.

Orbison sings of encountering an old flame and being overwhelmed by emotions, which move him to tears. While the lyrics convey deep sorrow and unbearable longing, it was Orbison's vocal performance in his distinctive tenor voice which really elevated the song as he showed off his ability to express complex emotions and vulnerability through his voice.

Displaying his unique style, the song and performance helped set a benchmark for vocal performance in the genre. His ability to hit the high notes with clarity is a hallmark of the song. And it wasn't just a production embellishment from the studio – Orbison's live performances of *Crying* were famous for their emotional intensity and vocal prowess, often leaving audiences in awe.

The single reached #2 in the US and #25 in the UK.

Check out these covers ...

US singer-songwriter Don McLean, of *American Pie* fame, had a major hit with his 1980 version which reached #1 on the UK Singles Chart and #5 on the US Billboard Hot 100.

A country version by Reba McEntire was well received and, in the same genre, Glen Campbell included his interpretation on his 1967 album *Gentle on My Mind*.

Then in 1987 Roy Orbison recorded the song again, this time as a duet with k.d. lang, which won a Grammy Award for Best Country Collaboration with Vocals.

REBA MCENTIRE

DON MCLEAN

GLEN CAMPBELL

HOTEL CALIFORNIA
THE EAGLES
1977

63

WRITTEN BY: Don Felder, Don Henley and Glenn Frey

RECORDED: March – October 1976

PRODUCER: Bill Szymczyk

ENGINEER: Allan Blazek, Bruce Hensal and Ed Mashal

RELEASED: 22 February 1977

Hotel California **by American rock band the Eagles continues to be a cornerstone of rock music, celebrated for its spellbinding lyrics, exceptional musicianship and enduring influence on the music industry.**

A track from the Eagles album of the same name, it is often interpreted as a commentary on the hedonism and excess of the 1970s American lifestyle, particularly in California. It is about a visitor to a luxury hotel who then discovers he can't leave it, with themes of excess, disillusionment and entrapment woven throughout the song.

It brought the Eagles huge critical acclaim and commercial success, winning the Grammy Award for Record of the Year in 1978, and remains a defining song of the band's career.

The song's intricate guitar work and memorable lyrics make it one of the foremost rock songs of all time, with the dual guitar solo by Don Felder and Joe Walsh often cited as one of the greatest in rock history. The pair take turns playing the lead, also harmonising and playing arpeggios before the fade out, in a two-minute and 12 seconds long guitar masterclass.

It peaked at #1 in the US and #8 in the UK, selling millions of copies worldwide as a single, while the album it is from is one of the best-selling of all time, certified 26× Platinum by the RIAA in the United States.

Check out these covers ...

A flamenco version by The Gipsy Kings gained popularity, especially after being featured in the film *The Big Lebowski*.

Etta James has also added her unique bluesy style to the song. The Eagles themselves have released several live versions as it's a staple of their concerts.

GIPSY KINGS

ETTA JAMES

CRAZY
PATSY CLINE
1961

62

WRITTEN BY: Willie Nelson

RECORDED: 21 August 1961

PRODUCER: Owen Bradley

ENGINEER: Glenn Snoddy and Harold Bradley

RELEASED: 16 October 1961

The most popular version of Crazy – a ballad about heartbreak and unrequited love – is a cover performed by American country music artist Patsy Cline.

The 'narrator' reflects on her feelings of sorrow and regret over a lost love, admitting to feeling 'crazy' for still loving the person, despite the heartache. The emotional depth and vulnerability in Cline's performance capture the song's poignant message giving her a huge hit and solidifying her position as a leading figure in country music. The song also broadened her audience by crossing over to the pop charts – one of the first country songs to make that move. It got to #2 in the country charts and #9 on the Billboard Hot 100. The track didn't chart in the UK at the time but has since gained recognition as a classic. Its producer and engineer Owen and Harold Bradley are credited with developing the 'Nashville Sound'.

Patsy Cline initially had difficulty recording the song due to her injuries from a car accident, but her perseverance resulted in her legendary vocal performance, which is still celebrated for its brilliance.

The song's writer Willie Nelson has recorded *Crazy* himself, and while it was not a major hit for him as a performer, it was a pivotal song in his career as a songwriter and contributed significantly to his later success as a country music recording artist. It is often cited as one of the greatest country songs ever written.

Check out these covers …

Aside from Willie Nelson's versions, including a duet with Julio Iglesias, highly regarded covers have been produced by Linda Ronstadt, LeAnn Rimes, Diana Krall and Michael Bublé, these last two adding a jazz element.

LINDA RONSTADT

LEANN RIMES

MICHAEL BUBLÉ

FAST CAR
TRACY CHAPMAN
1988

61

WRITTEN BY: Tracy Chapman

RECORDED: Late 1987

PRODUCER: David Kershenbaum

ENGINEER: Kevin W. Smith

RELEASED: 6 April 1988

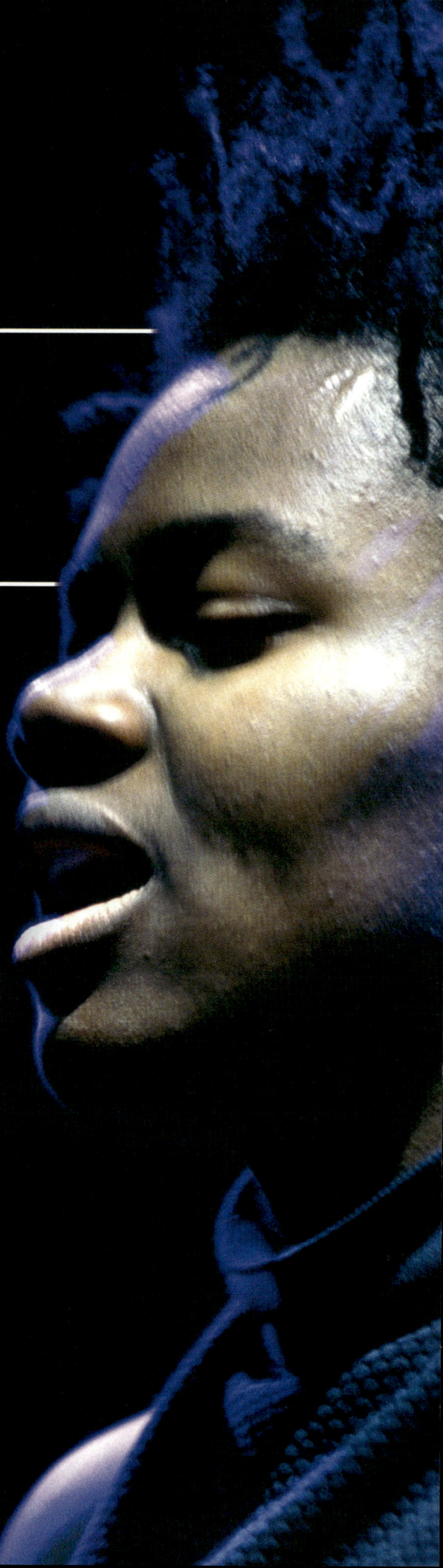

Tracy Chapman and her folk/rock song *Fast Car* shot to popularity after an unplanned performance she gave at a 70th birthday concert for Nelson Mandela at Wembley Stadium in 1988. She was scheduled to sing, lower on the bill, but when a technical hitch prevented Stevie Wonder from going on stage on time, Chapman was asked to fill in his much more prestigious slot. With just her guitar and a microphone, she won over the crowd with her tautly structured, poignant tale of struggle and hope.

Greeted with widespread critical acclaim, the song then took off to become a huge hit – reaching #4 in the UK and #6 in the US. As the lead single from her self-titled debut album it also helped Tracy Chapman win the 1989 Grammy Award for Best New Artist.

Fast Car enjoyed a resurgence in popularity in 2011 when Michael Collings performed a cover on *Britain's Got Talent*, leading to the original version re-entering the UK charts.

As a still relevant reflection on poverty, dreams of a better life and the challenges of escaping a difficult situation, *Fast Car* has endured as one of the greatest rock folk songs ever written.

Check out these covers ...

The song's enduring appeal was underlined in 2023 when American country music star Luke Combs scored a huge international hit with his version. This introduced a new generation to Tracy's songwriting talents and in 2023 she became the first black songwriter to win Song of the Year at the Country Music Awards some 35 years after her song's original release.

Other leading artists including Sam Smith, Justin Bieber, Kelly Clarkson and Chris Daughtry, have all shown their appreciation for the track by covering it during live performances.

The Blossoms produced a disco-flavoured version with a backbeat and synthesizer replacing the original guitar line. Known for their popular YouTube covers, Boyce Avenue's version of *Fast Car* has amassed millions of views. Their smooth, acoustic rendition helped bring the song to a broader, internet-savvy audience in 2009. Jonas Blue's 2015 cover with Dakota transformed *Fast Car* into a dance track which reached #2 in the UK and charted around the world including the US and Australia and making #1 in Europe and New Zealand.

LUKE COMBS

BLOSSOMS

A WHITER SHADE OF PALE
PROCOL HARUM
1967

60

WRITTEN BY: Gary Brooker (music), Keith Reid (lyrics), Matthew Fisher (organ part later acknowledged in court) and all members of the band

RECORDED: March 1967

PRODUCER: Denny Cordell

ENGINEER: Keith Grant

RELEASED: 12 May 1967

A *Whiter Shade of Pale* by the British rock band Procol Harum is one of the defining songs of the psychedelic rock era and famous for its distinctive organ riff and enigmatic lyrics.

The lyrics are noted for their surreal, poetic imagery, which has been subject to much interpretation. Including themes of love, loss and existential reflection, their precise meaning remains elusive, and has been interpreted in many different ways over the years.

The song's melancholic tone and baroque-pop sound create a dreamy, haunting atmosphere. Its unique blend of classical and rock elements set a new standard for psychedelic music and made it a defining track of the Summer of Love in 1967. The classical influence from the organ line, heavily inspired by Johann Sebastian Bach's *Air on the G String* adds to its baroque pop sound.

It was an immediate hit upon release when it made #1 in the UK and #5 in the US, selling over 10m copies worldwide.

Check out these covers ...

It has been covered extensively, one of the most notable coming from Annie Lennox on her album 1995 album *Medusa*. Joe Cocker included a version on his 1978 album *Luxury You Can Afford*, Willie Nelson featured it on his 1982 album *Always on my Mind* and Sarah Brightman covered it on her album *La Luna* in 2000.

ANNIE LENNOX

JOE COCKER

SARAH BRIGHTMAN

A CHANGE IS GONNA COME

SAM COOKE

1964

59

WRITTEN BY: Sam Cooke

RECORDED: December 1963

PRODUCER: Luigi Creatore and Hugo Peretti

ENGINEER: Al Schmitt

RELEASED: 22 December 1964

Inspired by American soul singer-songwriter Cooke's first-hand experiences with racism, *A Change Is Gonna Come* became an anthem for the struggle for civil rights in 1960s America.

The lyrics express a deep yearning for equality and justice, reflecting both personal pain and hope for societal change, and encapsulate the optimism and determination of the Civil Rights Movement. Cooke was inspired to write *A Change Is Gonna Come* after hearing Bob Dylan's *Blowin' in the Wind*, which motivated him to create a similar anthem for the African-American experience after he and his band were turned away from a whites-only motel.

Adding to the song's emotional and historical weight is the fact that it was released posthumously, shortly after Cooke's sudden death. Aged just 33, he was shot and killed by Bertha Franklin, the manager of the Hacienda Motel in Los Angeles, California under controversial and tragic circumstances on 11 December 1964.

. It is widely regarded as one of Cooke's most significant contributions to music having become emblematic of the struggle for racial equality.

Chartwise, it peaked at #31 on the US Billboard 100 and #9 on the Hot R&B Singles listing, although it didn't chart in the UK when first released.

Check out these covers ...

The song has influenced generations of musicians and activists and been covered frequently, including by Aretha Franklin whose rendition is one of the most acclaimed covers, as she adds her powerful voice to the song's legacy.

A version by Otis Redding brought a raw emotional intensity to the song, while Seal's 2004 version introduced the song to a new 21st century generation.

ARETHA FRANKLIN

OTIS REDDING

DREAMS
FLEETWOOD MAC
1977

58

WRITTEN BY: Stevie Nicks

RECORDED: Early 1977

PRODUCER: Lindsey Buckingham and Richard Dashut

ENGINEER: Ken Caillat

RELEASED: 24 March 1977

From their landmark album *Rumours*, released in February 1977, *Dreams* stands out as Fleetwood Mac's sole chart-topping hit in the United States where it reached #1 in June that year and sold over a million copies.

It was written by singer-songwriter Stevie Nicks during a tumultuous period for her and the other band members who were all going through personal upheavals at the time. Nicks relationship with the band's guitarist/vocalist/producer Lindsey Buckingham had broken down, fellow band

members Christine McVie and John McVie were separating and drummer and co-founder of the band Mick Fleetwood was going through a divorce.

Released as the second single from *Rumours*, *Dreams* is a quintessential example of the band's prowess in crafting emotionally resonant pop-rock anthems. It highlights a seamless fusion of poignant lyrics and melodies, and infectious rhythms. Stevie Nicks' distinctive vocals, layered over a hypnotic bassline and steady drumbeat, convey a sense of longing and vulnerability. Its timeless appeal continues to captivate audiences, making it a staple of classic rock radio and one of the band's best-loved hits.

Check out these covers ...

One of the most famous covers of *Dreams* is by Irish band The Corrs, who released their widely acclaimed version in 1998 on their album *Talk on Corners*. The Corrs' rendition stayed true to the original while adding their own signature Celtic instrumentation and helped introduce Fleetwood Mac's music to a new generation of listeners.

THE CORRS

(I CAN'T GET NO) SATISFACTION

THE ROLLING STONES

1965

57

WRITTEN BY: Mick Jagger and Keith Richards

RECORDED: May 1965

PRODUCER: Andrew Loog Oldham

ENGINEER: Dave Hassinger

RELEASED: 6 June 1965 (US) and 20 August 1965 (UK)

One of the Rolling Stones' most famous hits, *(I Can't Get No) Satisfaction* gave the band their first American #1, propelling them to even greater international fame and cementing their status as one of the greatest rock bands of all time.

The pre-eminent British rock group since their first UK #1 hit *It's All Over Now* in July 1964, the Rolling Stones revolutionised rock music thanks in no small part to the talents of Mick Jagger and Keith Richards, the band's principal songwriting duo, who played integral roles in shaping the band's sound and aesthetic.

Lauded as the most magnetic frontman in rock, Jagger's charismatic stage presence and distinctive vocal delivery, was teamed with a knack for crafting memorable and evocative lyrics. This song was a blistering commentary on

consumerism, materialism and the relentless pursuit of gratification in post-war Western society. The song's infectious melody and memorable chorus became an instant rallying cry for a generation disillusioned with the trappings of modern life and feeling alienated by the relentless bombardment of advertising and societal expectations.

Jagger's defiant vocal delivery created a sense of urgency and rebellion and the track's raw energy was underpinned by Keith Richards and Ronnie Wood together riding raucous guitar riffs, alongside Charlie Watts setting the pace on drums. Together the band crafted an enduring anthem of disillusionment and cultural critique, emblematic of their own impact on the popular music landscape.

With controversial lyrics, including overt references to sexual frustration and social dissatisfaction, *(I Can't Get No) Satisfaction* sparked debate about censorship and cemented The Rolling Stones' reputation as 1960s 'bad boys' – provocateurs and cultural icons.

Check out these covers ...

Among the many covers of the song, American new wave band Devo released a version on their debut album *Q: Are We Not Men? A: We Are Devo!* in 1978, including electronic elements and quirky vocals.

Then Britney Spears gave the song a contemporary pop makeover on her second studio album *Oops! ... I Did It Again* in 2000.

That same year, Indie rock artist Cat Power recorded a powerful, stripped-down version of *(I Can't Get No) Satisfaction* for her album *The Covers*.

DEVO

BRITNEY SPEARS

CAT POWER

MY GENERATION
THE WHO
1965

56

WRITTEN BY: Pete Townshend
RECORDED: 13 October 1965
PRODUCER: Shel Talmy
ENGINEER: Glyn Johns
RELEASED: Oct 1965 (UK) and Nov 1965 (US)

M*y Generation* is widely regarded as one of the most influential songs of the 1960s.

As an anthem of youthful rebellion and defiance, the lyrics express the frustrations and desires of the younger generation, famously including the line 'Hope I die before I get old', which captured the ethos of the 1960s counterculture. The song's raw energy and aggressive sound mirrored the feelings of disillusionment and resistance prevalent among the youth at the time.

Raw, energetic and bold, it was immediately adopted by the mod subculture. Roger Daltrey's stuttering delivery of the lyrics was originally intended to mimic the speech pattern of a mod on amphetamines and is a distinctive feature of the song. The song also features a notable bass solo by John Entwistle, which was groundbreaking at the time.

A track from The Who's best-selling album of the same name, it went on to become a defining song of the era, peaking at #2 on the UK Singles Chart and #74 on the Billboard Hot 100.

Check out these covers ...

Patti Smith gave the song a punk twist when she included a cover on her 1975 debut album *Horses (Legacy Edition)*.

Rock-orientated interpretations include Iron Maiden who covered the song as a B-side to their single *Lord of the Flies* in 1995.

Less predictably, Hilary Duff released a pop cover in 2004 and a group of senior citizens performing as The Zimmers reached #26 on the UK Singles Chart in 2007.

Several bands have included *My Generation* in their live shows paying homage to The Who as major influences, including Oasis, Pearl Jam, MC5 and Green Day.

IRON MAIDEN

PATTI SMITH

HILARY DUFF

PAPA'S GOT A BRAND NEW BAG

JAMES BROWN

1965

55

WRITTEN BY: James Brown

RECORDED: February 1965

PRODUCER: James Brown

ENGINEER: Ron Lenhoff

RELEASED: June 1965

***Papa's Got a Brand New Bag* is one of James Brown's most influential songs, and often credited with helping to create the whole genre of 'funk'.**

The song is a celebration of a man who has discovered a new sense of style and confidence. The song's protagonist, Papa, has adopted a new dance style and a fresh outlook, as the phrase 'brand new bag' means a new way of doing things, a fresh approach.

Significant for its groundbreaking use of rhythm which had a lasting impact on music, the song features a strong emphasis on the first beat of each measure, known as 'on the one', a characteristic that became a hallmark of James Brown's music and funk in general.

The original recording was sped up slightly for the final release, which gave it a slightly higher pitch and a more energetic feel. The single was released in two parts, with *Papa's Got a Brand New Bag (Part 1)* and *Papa's Got a Brand New Bag (Part 2)* on the B-side.

As well as influencing countless artists and bands, the song marked a turning point in James Brown's career, establishing him as a major force in popular music, an innovator of the funk genre and securing his status as the 'Godfather of Soul'. It also won him his first Grammy Award for Best Rhythm & Blues Recording in 1966.

The song reached #8 on the Billboard Hot 100, #1 on the Billboard R&B Singles chart, and #25 in the UK.

Check out these covers …

Otis Redding's 1968 cover brought a soulful and more laid-back interpretation of the song. Other '60s covers were produced by blues guitarist and singer Buddy Guy, and also The Fabulous Echoes who brought the song to the Hong Kong music scene.

OTIS REDDING

BUDDY GUY

THE FABULOUS ECHOES

JOHNNY B. GOODE
CHUCK BERRY
1958

54

WRITTEN BY: Chuck Berry

RECORDED: 6 January 1958

PRODUCER: Leonard Chess and Phil Chess

ENGINEER: Uncredited team from Chess Records

RELEASED: 31 March 1958

With one of rock's immortal melodies and what would become trademark guitar licks, *Johnny B. Goode* was written and recorded by Chuck Berry, one of the founding fathers of rock and roll who was instrumental in taking R&B music in a new direction. This pioneering track lyrically embraced the issues of the burgeoning teenage market, while musically merging hillbilly country, urban blues and hot jazz styles through an electric guitar, in a seemingly effortless 'pickin' style.

The song tells the story of a young country boy with dreams of becoming a famous guitar player. The protagonist, Johnny, is described as a poor but talented musician whose guitar skills have the potential to make him a star. The song is often interpreted as semi-autobiographical, reflecting Berry's own experiences and aspirations.

Although it wasn't his highest-charting hit, *Johnny B. Goode* has gone on to become the most iconic and enduring of Chuck Berry's work.

Michael J. Fox, Back To The Future, 1985

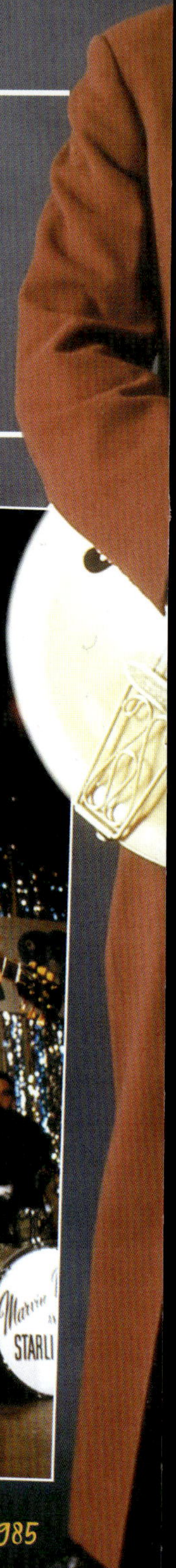

Check out these covers ...

As befits one of the greatest rock and roll songs of all time, Johnny B. Goode has been covered in live performances by many of the greatest rock and roll artists who have followed in Chuck Berry's wake, including Jimi Hendrix, Elvis Presley, The Beatles, Coldplay, AC/DC, Green Day and Judas Priest.

Jamaican musician Peter Tosh released a reggae version of Johnny B. Goode in 1983, showcasing the song's versatility across genres. The song enjoyed a further burst of popularity in the 1980s when it was featured in the hit film *Back to the Future*, when lead character Marty McFly who has time-travelled from 1985 sings the song at a high school prom in 1955, three years before the song was actually a hit.

JIMI HENDRIX

AC/DC

Fun fact

Johnny B. Goode was selected for inclusion on the Voyager Golden Record, which was sent into space aboard the Voyager spacecraft in 1977, as a representation of Earth's music.

GREEN DAY

WITH OR WITHOUT YOU

U2

1987

53

WRITTEN BY: Bono, The Edge, Adam Clayton and Larry Mullen Jr.

RECORDED: During 1986/87

PRODUCER: Brian Eno and Daniel Lanois

ENGINEER: Mark Ellis, Dave Meegan and Pat McCarthy

RELEASED: 16 March 1987

By marrying lyrics with a social and political edge to anthemic production, U2 carved out a special space in stadium rock in the 1980s. *With or Without You*, the lead single from their fifth studio album, 1987's *The Joshua Tree*, solidified the band's status as leading players in the rock scene by providing them with their first US #1.

Regularly cited as one of U2's finest songs, the ballad has received widespread critical acclaim for its emotional depth, minimalist production, Bono's passionate vocal performance and The Edge's distinctive guitar riff.

As well as topping the US Billboard Hot 100 for three weeks, it also reached #1 in Canada and Ireland and #4 on the UK Singles Chart.

Its powerful lyrics, sung so distinctively by Bono, were said to have been inspired by his own struggle to balance his family life with his career as a rock star.

The song is also notable for its use of the Infinite Guitar – a modified electric guitar invented by Michael Brook – which allows for notes to be sustained indefinitely. This added to the song's atmospheric and ethereal sound.

Check out these covers ...

Unusual but arresting versions of *With or Without You* have been produced by Belgian girls' choir Scala & Kolacny Brothers, and the Croatian cellist duo 2Cellos who released an instrumental version on their debut album in 2011.

2CELLOS

SCALA & KOLACNY BROTHERS

HEARTBREAK HOTEL
ELVIS PRESLEY
1956

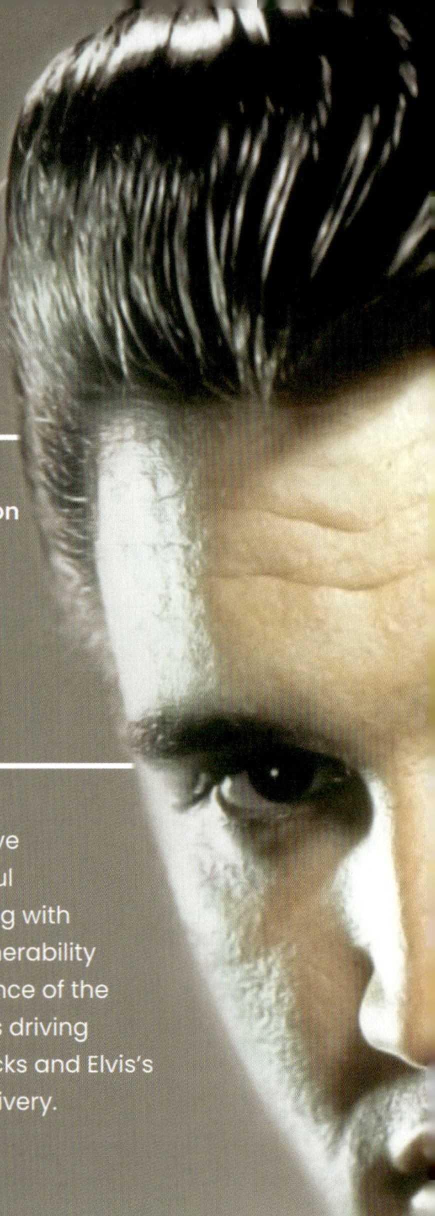

52

WRITTEN BY: Tommy Durden and Mae Boren Axton

RECORDED: 10 January 1956

PRODUCER: Steve Sholes

ENGINEER: Bob Ferris

RELEASED: 27 January 1956

Following his move to RCA in 1955, Elvis Presley broke through to international stardom and scored the first of his 18 #1 hits with the seminal *Heartbreak Hotel* in 1956.

Legend goes that its lyrics were inspired by a newspaper article about the suicide of a young man who jumped from a hotel window. The song was certainly gloomy and other singers had turned it down, including the Wilburn Brothers who thought it was 'strange and almost morbid'.

Giving Elvis his first million-seller, the song topped the Billboard 100 chart for seven weeks, the Cashbox singles chart for six weeks and the Country and Western Chart for 17 weeks. It also made number three on the R&B chart. As well as propelling Elvis to instant stardom, the song made an incredible impact on many of the mega-star musicians who would follow in his wake, including The Beatles. Paul McCartney described the recording as nothing less than the most important artistic creation of the modern era.

More than just a hit song, "Heartbreak Hotel" was a cultural phenomenon that helped define the sound and spirit of rock and roll music and make Elvis its 'King'. His emotive performance and soulful delivery infused the song with a raw intensity and vulnerability captured the very essence of the rockabilly sound with its driving rhythm, bluesy guitar licks and Elvis's unmistakable vocal delivery.

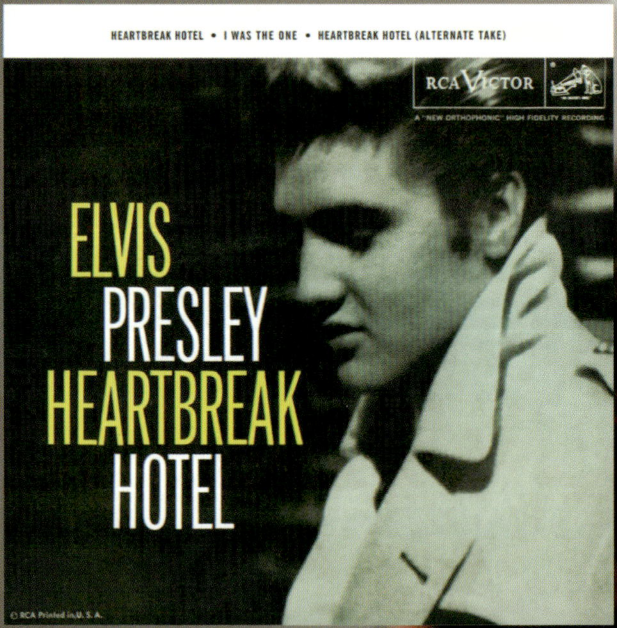

Check out these covers ...

Many artists have reinterpreted *Heartbreak Hotel* including Connie Francis, Willie Nelson and John Cale, a founding member of the Velvet Underground.

CONNIE FRANCIS

WILLIE NELSON

JOHN CALE

BROWN EYED GIRL
VAN MORRISON

1967

51

WRITTEN BY: Van Morrison

RECORDED: 28 March 1967

PRODUCER: Bert Berns

ENGINEER: Brooks Arthur

RELEASED: June 1967

Van Morrison's debut single, a masterpiece reflection on love and longing, was inspired by the American and jazz blues music he was exposed to while growing up in Belfast, Northern Ireland. Van's innate talent for poetic imagery and transcendent vocals went on to forge a visionary new sound in popular music.

Brown Eyed Girl is a timeless fusion of rock, R&B and folk influences which featured on his first solo studio album, *Blowin' Your Mind.* It has since received millions of hours of airplay, despite the fact that Van himself never rated the song and believes he has written hundreds of songs that are better.

But as a celebration of youth, nostalgia and the simple joys of life *Brown Eyed Girl* has continued to resonate with listeners over the years. Its catchy melody, infectious groove and evocative lyrics paint a vivid picture of carefree summer days and youthful romance.

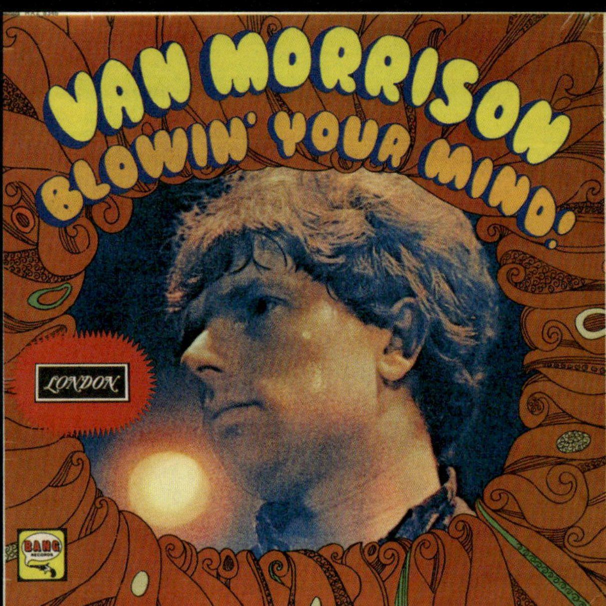

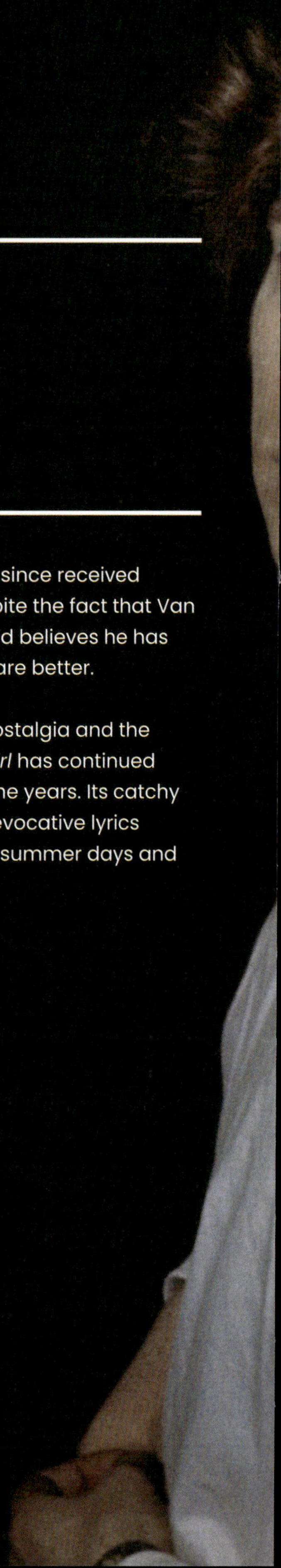

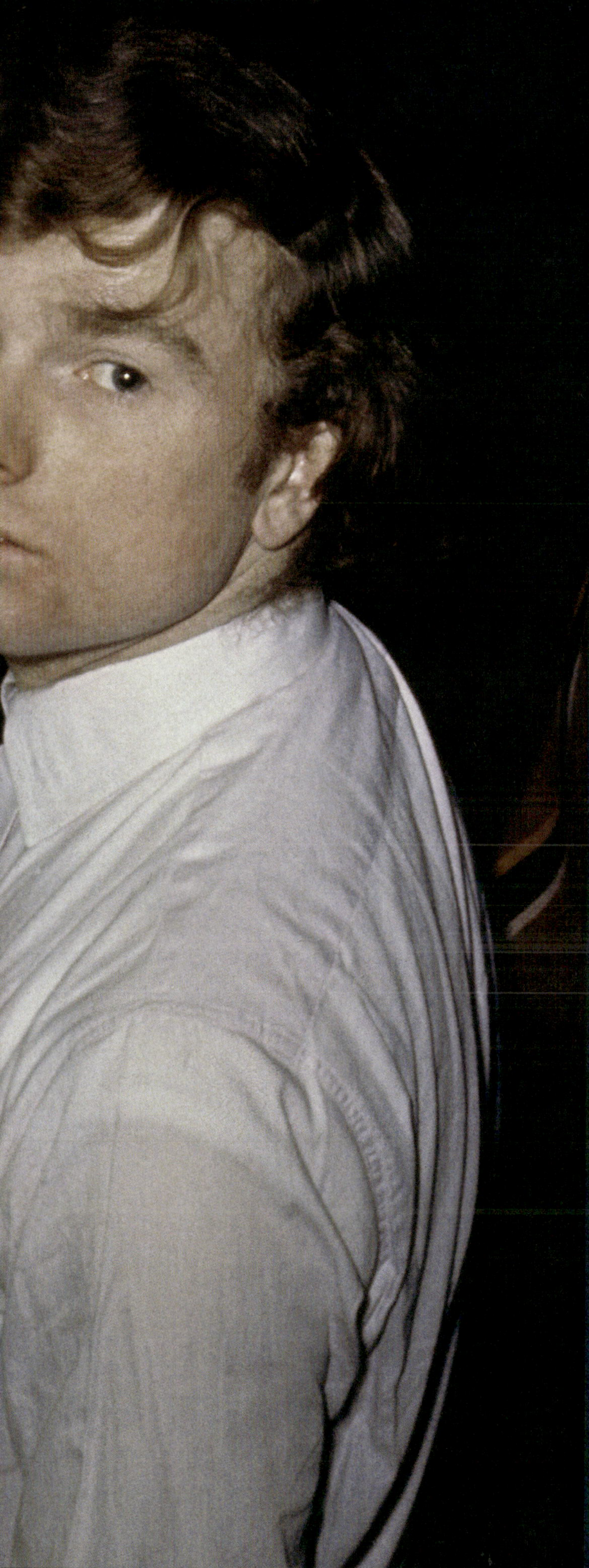

Check out these covers ...

The song has been performed by many artists over the years and was recorded by American singer-songwriter Jimmy Buffett who added a tropical flavour complete with steel drums, acoustic guitars and breezy harmonies on his *One Particular Harbor* album.

JIMMY BUFFETT

I WILL SURVIVE
GLORIA GAYNOR
1978

50

WRITTEN BY: Freddie Perren and Dino Fekaris

RECORDED: 1978

PRODUCER: Freddie Perren

ENGINEER: Ben Holland, John Matousek and Chris Michie

RELEASED: 23 October 1978

With its timeless message of self-empowerment and resilience, set to an energetic beat, *I Will Survive* is still celebrated as a feminist anthem, as well as being a staple of the disco music scene.

Initially released as the B-side to Gaynor's song *Substitute*, DJs began playing it more frequently than the A side so that it gained an eventual re-release as an A-side in its own right.

The song received widespread critical acclaim for its catchy melody, Gaynor's powerful vocal performance, and its early 'Girl Power' message.

It reached #1 on the Billboard Hot 100 chart in March 1979 and was also a #1 hit on the Billboard Hot Dance Club Play chart, eventually being certified Platinum by the RIAA. Its success was duplicated in the UK, where it was also a #1 hit in 1979, and around the world where it sold millions of copies.

On top of this sales success, the song won the first and only Grammy Award for Best Disco Recording in 1980, after which the category was discontinued.

It went on to become a cultural phenomenon, embraced by various social movements and individuals, particularly by the LGBTQ+ community, as a declaration of strength and defiance.

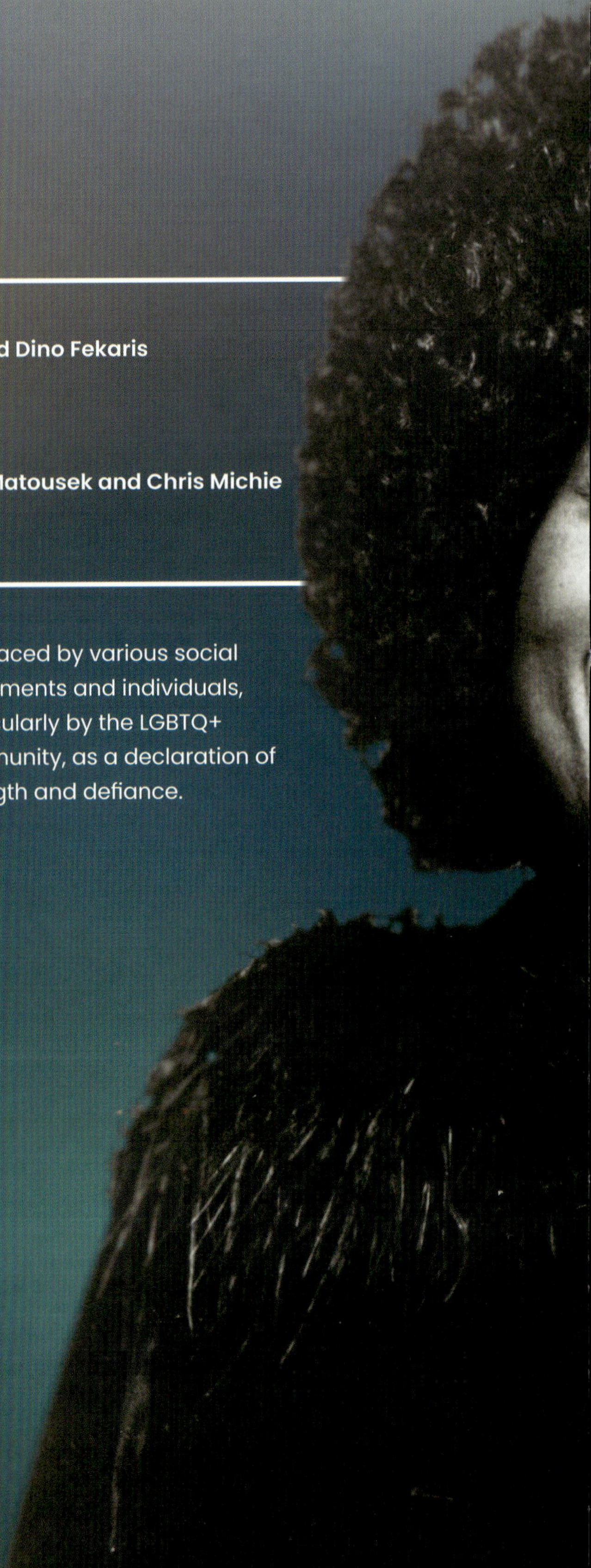

Check out these covers ...

Diana Ross performed a cover on her 1995 album *Take Me Higher* and Gladys Knight gave her soulful version in 1996 on her album *Many Different Roads.*

Dutch pop group Hermes House Band released a dance version in 1994 that became a hit in Europe and Chantay Savage's slowed-down R&B version in 1996 reached #12 on the Billboard Hot 100.

Pussycat Dolls and Demi Lovato have modernised the song when covering it in their live performances.

DIANA ROSS

GLADYS KNIGHT

DEMI LOVATO

PUSSYCAT DOLLS

BORN TO RUN
BRUCE SPRINGSTEEN
1975

49

WRITTEN BY: Bruce Springsteen

RECORDED: May – June 1975

PRODUCER: Bruce Springsteen and Mike Appel

ENGINEER: Louis Lahav

RELEASED: 25 August 1975

American rock musician Bruce Springsteen – The Boss – got his career breakthrough with *Born to Run*, the title track from his third studio album, and now his signature song.

In true Springsteen style, it's about the yearning for freedom and a better life – and, of course, references a motorbike. The lyrics tell the story of a young couple, often interpreted as Springsteen and a girlfriend (Wendy in the song), who dream of leaving their town to find a place where they can live freely and happily.

It influenced the rock genre significantly, setting a new standard for rock and roll with its grandeur and thematic depth.

The recording of *Born to Run* was meticulous, with Springsteen striving for a 'wall of sound' production style which involved laying down multiple tracks. It took months to perfect. Including flawless backing by his E Street Band, *Born to Run* was a breakthrough for Springsteen, gaining extensive radio play which catapulted him into the mainstream success he's enjoyed ever since.

The song peaked at #23 on the Billboard chart to give Springsteen his first Top 40 hit, and although the song didn't do as well outside the US at the time, it has since grown to be a monster hit worldwide.

Check out these covers ...

As Springsteen's 'most performed' song in concert – with some ritual around its performance – there's not a lot of incentive for others to take on this towering track.

However, check out the version by Allan Clarke, lead singer with the British '60s band the Hollies. This was actually the first recording of the song, although its release was delayed, only appearing after Springsteen's own version.

Another interesting cover can be found on Frankie Goes to Hollywood's 1984 album *Welcome to the Pleasuredome* and singer Suzi Quatro has also put her spin on the track.

ALLAN CLARKE

SUZI QUATRO

Fun fact

The *Born to Run* album cover, featuring Springsteen leaning on saxophonist Clarence Clemons, is considered one of the greatest rock album covers of all time.

WONDERWALL
OASIS
1995

48

WRITTEN BY: Noel Gallagher

RECORDED: May 1995

PRODUCER: Owen Morris and Noel Gallagher

ENGINEER: Owen Morris

RELEASED: 30 October 1995

Manchester rock band Oasis, led by brothers Noel and Liam Gallagher, rose to fame and became a defining band of the Britpop era with their debut album *Definitely Maybe.* Their 1995 follow up album *(What's the Story) Morning Glory?*, featuring *Wonderwall* solidified their success and intensified their rivalry with London's Britpop band Blur.

With an anthemic and powerful chorus, separating calmer more reflective verses, *Wonderwall* is considered the band's signature song and one of the most recognisable and successful songs of the 1990s overall.

It peaked at #2 on the UK Singles Chart, where it has sold 2.8 million copies, making it the second biggest selling UK single never to make it to #1, after Robson and Jerome's track *I Believe* beat off its challenge. By April 2022 it was certified six times platinum, equating to sales of over 3,600,000 in the UK alone.

And by reaching #8 on the Billboard Hot 100, it became one of the band's most successful singles in the US.

Wonderwall was nominated for Best Rock Vocal Performance by a Duo or Group at the 1997 Grammy Awards and is one of the most streamed songs from the 1990s on platforms like Spotify, with hundreds of millions of streams. The song features a distinctive opening by Noel on acoustic guitar and goes on to include a string section, giving the song its rich and layered sound. Liam's raw and emotive lead vocals are the other standout feature of the song.

While the title 'Wonderwall' was inspired by George Harrison's 1968 solo album *Wonderwall Music*, the song's meaning is less obvious, though it has most often been interpreted as a reflection on relationships, longing and emotional introspection.

Check out these covers ...

In 1995, The Mike Flowers Pops released a retro easy listening version of *Wonderwall* that reached # 2 on the UK Singles Chart, humorously close to the original's peak position.

However, the 2003 cover of *Wonderwall* by American rock and country star Ryan Adams received critical acclaim and high praise from Noel Gallagher, who said he preferred it to his original.

Cat Power's stripped-down version of the song was also well received in 2000 and boyband One Direction covered *Wonderwall* during their early tours from 2011, introducing the song to a new generation of fans.

RYAN ADAMS

CAT POWER

I WILL ALWAYS LOVE YOU
WHITNEY HOUSTON
1992

47

WRITTEN BY: Dolly Parton

RECORDED: 1992

PRODUCER: David Foster

ENGINEER: Mick Guzauski

RELEASED: 3 November 1992

This is another fine example of a cover outdoing the original. This time it was American singer and actress Whitney Houston who took this Dolly Parton original to new heights. The heights were almost literal as Whitney's version features a dramatic key change towards the end, signalling the emotional climax of the song. Her performance during this section is simply breathtaking, demonstrating her unparalleled vocal prowess. Her remarkable vocal range and control was further showcased at the beginning of the song which she opened up with a powerful a cappella section.

While Dolly Parton's original version of *I Will Always Love You*, released in 1973, was a country lament, Whitney Houston's rendition transformed it into a soulful, R&B-infused power ballad.

The immense popularity of the song was bolstered by its inclusion in the soundtrack of Whitney's 1992 hit movie *The Bodyguard*, which also became one of the best-selling soundtracks in history.

This helped the song's unprecedented success, breaking numerous records and becoming one of the best-selling singles of all time, shifting some 20 million copies. It won two Grammy Awards, including Record of the Year, and remains one of the best-selling singles by a female artist. Commercially it topped the Billboard Hot 100 chart for 14 weeks, making it one of the longest-running number-one singles in history at the time. It also reached #1 on the UK Singles Chart, where it stayed for 10 weeks.

It's a breakup song, but perhaps more of a farewell than a tale of heartbreak. Dolly Parton, who received huge royalties from Whitney's version, described it as 'a simple little song that's about everything and nothing'.

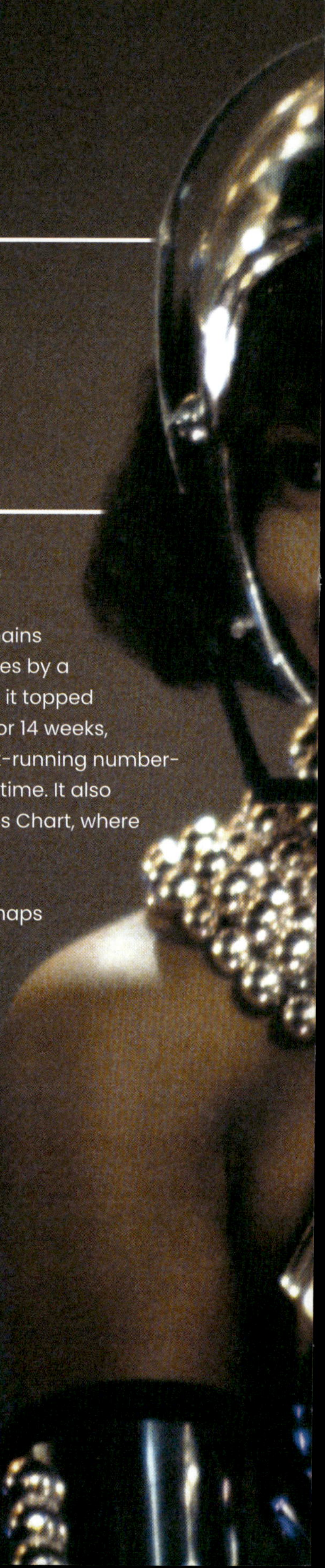

Check out these covers ...

While countless artists have covered *I Will Always Love You*, few have matched the success and acclaim of Whitney Houston's rendition. However, notably accomplished covers include those by Linda Ronstadt, LeAnn Rimes and Jennifer Hudson.

JENNIFER HUDSON

LINDA RONSTADT

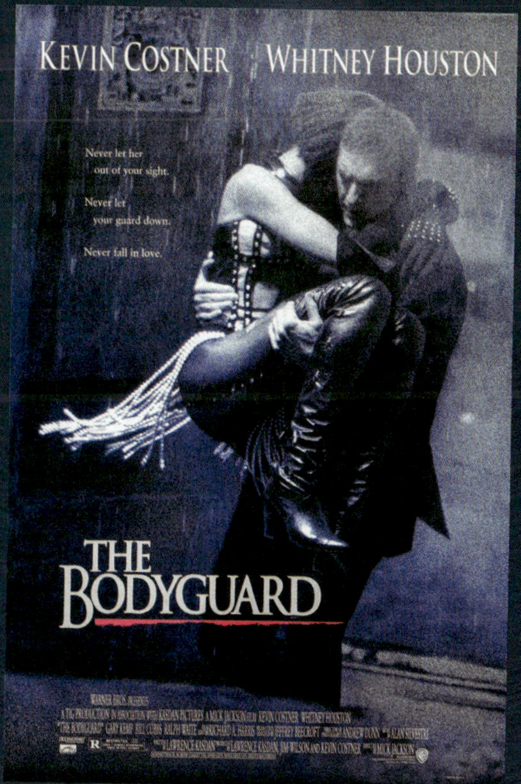

THAT'LL BE THE DAY
BUDDY HOLLY

1957

46

WRITTEN BY: Buddy Holly, Jerry Allison and Norman Petty

RECORDED: 25 February 1957

PRODUCER: Norman Petty

ENGINEER: Norman Petty

RELEASED: 27 May 1957

This peppy track has a prominent place in music history as one of the pioneering works of rock and roll. It was created and performed by one of rock music's first singer-songwriter-guitarists, Buddy Holly, who had a brief but dazzling career before his premature death in a plane crash in 1959 when he was just 22 years old. A central figure in the development of mid-50s rock and roll, Buddy had a distinctive vocal style incorporating little hiccoughs and falsetto, which he used to full effect on *That'll Be the Day* which topped the American and British singles charts.

At its core, the song is a defiant declaration of independence and self-assurance which exploded onto the music scene, resonating with teenagers eager to embrace a new sound and attitude. Its infectious melody, catchy lyrics and energetic rhythm embodied the essence of rock and roll, and it became an instant hit.

Encapsulating youthful defiance and a determination to live life to the full, Buddy's raw vocal delivery amplified this spirit, while the driving beat of the music made it impossible to resist tapping a foot or joining in on the chorus. With infectious energy and timeless appeal, this Buddy Holly masterpiece will forever stand as a symbol of rebellion, freedom and the enduring power of rock and roll.

Check out these covers ...

Several artists have covered *That'll Be the Day* over the years, including British rock band The Quarrymen, which included a young John Lennon, Paul McCartney and George Harrison. Although their version was a homemade recording and never commercially released at the time, it has gained historical significance as one of the earliest recordings featuring members of what would later become The Beatles and provides insight into their musical roots.

Close harmony pop duo Don and Phil Everly, known as The Everly Brothers had a hit with their version of *That'll Be the Day* in December 1964. But one of the most successful cover versions was by American rock singer Linda Ronstadt, who included the song on her 1976 album *Hasten Down the Wind*. Her rock-infused arrangement reached the Top 20 on the Billboard Hot 100 chart and received widespread acclaim from both fans and critics alike.

THE QUARRYMEN

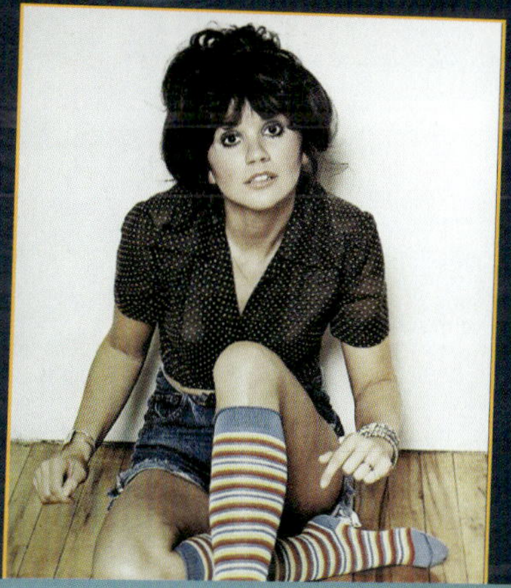

LINDA RONSTADT

THE EVERLY BROTHERS

LAYLA

DEREK AND THE DOMINOS

1970

45

WRITTEN BY: Eric Clapton and Jim Gordon

RECORDED: August and September 1970

PRODUCER: Tom Dowd

ENGINEER: Ron Albert and Chuck Kirkpatrick

RELEASED: November 1970

L*ayla* is famously inspired by Eric Clapton's unrequited love for Pattie Boyd, the wife of his friend and fellow musician George Harrison of The Beatles. The song's lyrics express Clapton's deep feelings of longing and despair over this impossible love. The title 'Layla' is derived from the Middle Eastern tale of Layla and Majnun, a classic story of doomed love, although in real life Clapton and Boyd did marry eventually.

The song is still celebrated for its passionate lyrics, emotive vocal delivery and especially its iconic guitar riff and coda. The latter part, a piano piece by Jim Gordon, adds a unique and unexpected dimension to the song.

First released in November 1970 as part of the album *Layla and Other Assorted Love Songs* by Derek and the Dominos, it was also released as a single in 1971. Yet despite its now-legendary status, *Layla* initially had only modest chart success, peaking at #51 on the Billboard Hot 100 in 1971. However, the 1972 re-release reached #10.

Although this period of work is frequently referred to as the pinnacle of Clapton's career, his time in the blues/rock outfit Derek and the Dominos was short. He formed the band in early 1970 but plagued by issues revolving around personal conflicts, substance abuse and professional struggles, the band was finished by 1971.

Nevertheless, Clapton has performed *Layla* in various formats throughout his career, including acoustic renditions, most notably for the MTV Unplugged series in 1992. This acoustic version won a Grammy Award for Best Rock Song.

Check out these covers ...

Covers of this classic rock staple are surprisingly rare, and tend to be instrumental versions, smooth jazz or swing renditions, several seemingly inspired by Eric Clapton's MTV Unplugged version. Two worth a spin are by the Charlie Daniels Band and by Caribbean singer Henri Salvador.

HENRI SALVADOR

CHARLIE DANIELS

PURPLE RAIN
PRINCE
1984

44

WRITTEN BY: Prince

RECORDED: August 1983

PRODUCER: Prince and the Revolution

ENGINEER: David Leonard

RELEASED: 26 September 1984

***Purple Rain* served as the title track for Prince's album and the accompanying film of the same name. Clocking in at over eight minutes, *Purple Rain* features an expansive structure that includes multiple verses, choruses and instrumental breaks. The song builds to a climactic finale with Prince's renowned guitar solo, which he performed live during the recording and is listed among the very greatest in rock history.**

Showcasing his virtuosity and musical genius, the film itself is a seminal piece of 1980s cinema serving both as a musical drama and a vehicle for Prince's artistic vision. Set in Minneapolis, Minnesota, the action follows 'The Kid,' a talented but troubled musician played by Prince, as he navigates the music scene and struggles with personal demons.

Exploring themes of love, ambition and redemption, the film culminates in a climactic performance at the First Avenue nightclub when Prince gives his electrifying performance of *Purple Rain*, with impassioned vocals over the soaring melody. He's so into his craft at that point that it's as if he put his DNA into the song as he leads his listeners along to the lyric 'let me guide you'. Following his death in 2016, aged just 57, the song has taken on a hymn-like quality with its drum beat sounding out like a funeral dirge. It has continued to gain popularity as it is celebrated for its emotional depth and for tackling the universal themes of love, loss and loneliness.

Chartwise, it peaked at #2 on the Billboard Hot 100 and reached #8 on the UK Singles Chart. But it's another of those songs where sales alone don't account for its impact and influence.

Check out these covers ...

Among the artists with the musical guts to tackle such a classic are Stevie Wonder and Madonna, Culture Club, Bruce Springsteen and Corey Taylor of Slipknot and Stone Sour fame.

CULTURE CLUB

MADONNA

COREY TAYLOR

Purple Rain movie poster

WATERLOO SUNSET
THE KINKS
1967

43

WRITTEN BY: Ray Davies
RECORDED: April 1967
PRODUCER: Ray Davies
ENGINEER: Alan MacKenzie
RELEASED: 5 May 1967

This contemplative and poetic anthem to London is said to have begun life as a commentary on the Merseybeat sound which had emerged from Liverpool. But once The Beatles released *Penny Lane* (about a place in Liverpool), Ray Davies reworked his lyrics and it's now hard to imagine this love letter to London commemorating anywhere else.

Ray Davies has mentioned various inspirations for *Waterloo Sunset*. Commonly agreed to have been influenced by his love of London and its landmarks, Waterloo Bridge and the River Thames especially, other interpretations suggest it reflects Davies' personal experiences and the sense of isolation and longing he felt during that time.

The 'Terry and Julie' characters featured were widely thought to be film stars Terence Stamp and Julie Christie who were hugely famous and romantically involved during the 1960s. However, other references mention that he modelled those people on his own relatives, with Julie being his sister imagined to be going away with a boyfriend and feeling nostalgic for the home and times she would leave behind. It wouldn't be the only time Davies would feature his siblings in his music – most famously his older sister Rene inspired the 1982 single *Come Dancing*.

Whoever they were, Terry and Julie have passed into musical

legend as 'stars' of a now legendary song praised for its melodic beauty, lyrical depth, vivid imagery and melancholic yet uplifting tone. Moments of quiet introspection are juxtaposed with soaring choruses, creating a sense of ebb and flow throughout the track, just like the River Thames itself. And of course the guitar riff which opens the track is instantly recognisable.

The song is also notable for being the first to be produced by Ray Davies and the first Kinks song in true stereo sound. Davies has said the song is one of his personal favourites and he sang it at the closing ceremony of the London Olympics in 2012.

Check out these covers ...

The song has been covered by British rock band Def Leppard who included the track on their 2006 album *Yeah!*, which features a collection of the band's favourite cover songs from the 1960s and 1970s. Peter Gabriel included it on his 2010 *Scratch My Back (Special Edition)* album.

1960s model turned musical actress Twiggy featured the song on her 2011 album *Romantically Yours*.

PETER GABRIEL

TWIGGY

NOTHING COMPARES 2U
SINEAD O'CONNOR

1990

42

WRITTEN BY: Prince

RECORDED: 1989

PRODUCER: Nellee Hooper and Chris Birkett

ENGINEER: Chris Birkett

RELEASED: 8 January 1990

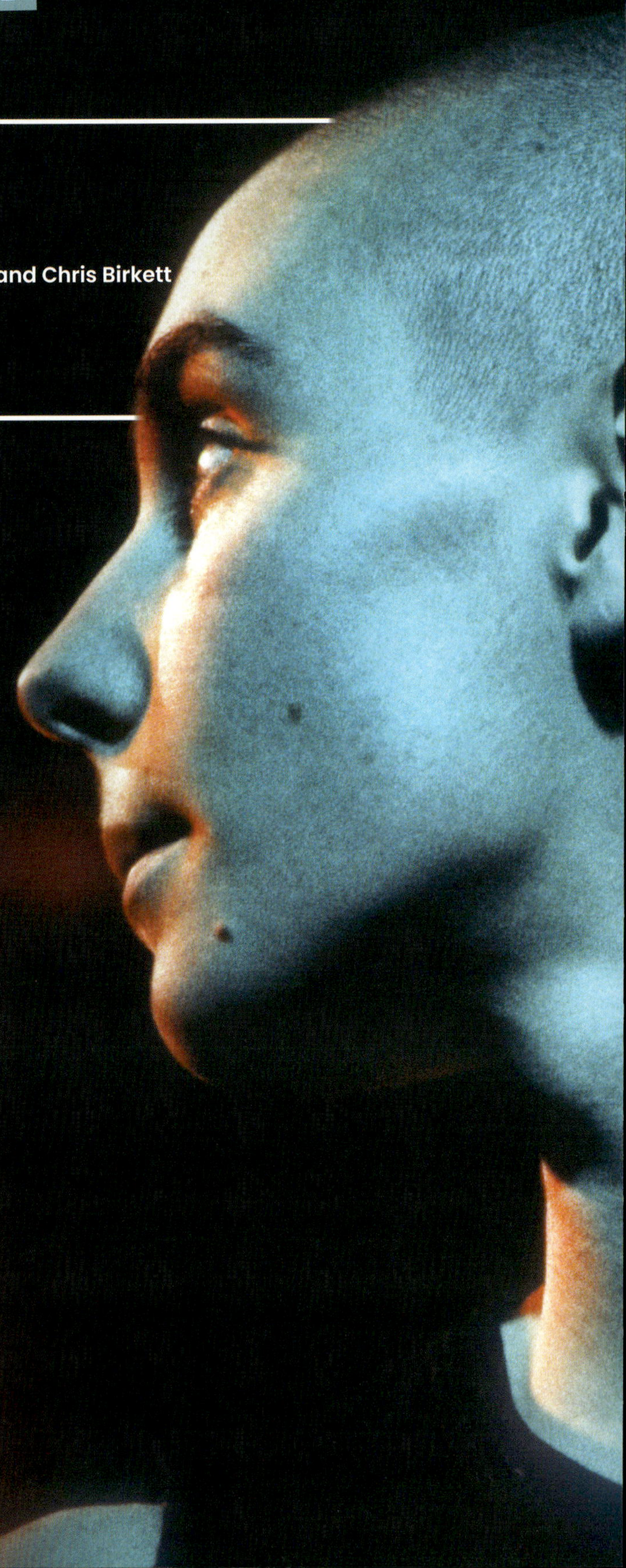

Irish musician Sinéad O'Connor became an international star with her cover of *Nothing Compares 2U* which she made her own, totally eclipsing the original version. Her achievement is all the greater because the song was originally written by the legendary artist Prince who first recorded it in 1985 with his side project, The Family, featuring members of his backing band, The Revolution, and other musicians.

However, the song did not achieve significant commercial success at the time and only became a hit when it was released as a single from Sinéad O'Connor's second studio album, *I Do Not Want What I Haven't Got.*

This version – with a completely different treatment and arrangement – reached #1 on the Billboard Hot 100 and the UK Singles Chart, staying at the top for four weeks on both sides of the Atlantic and catapulting Sinéad O'Connor to worldwide fame.

Her powerful and emotional interpretation of the song was captured in a now iconic accompanying video, directed by John Maybury, that focused almost entirely on her face, during which she shed a real tear as she sang. The video undoubtedly played a huge part in the success of this version, which sold millions of copies and topped charts around the world. Despite this success, and the songwriting royalties he would receive, there were reports that Prince was not entirely pleased with O'Connor's version. They reportedly had a contentious relationship regarding the song.

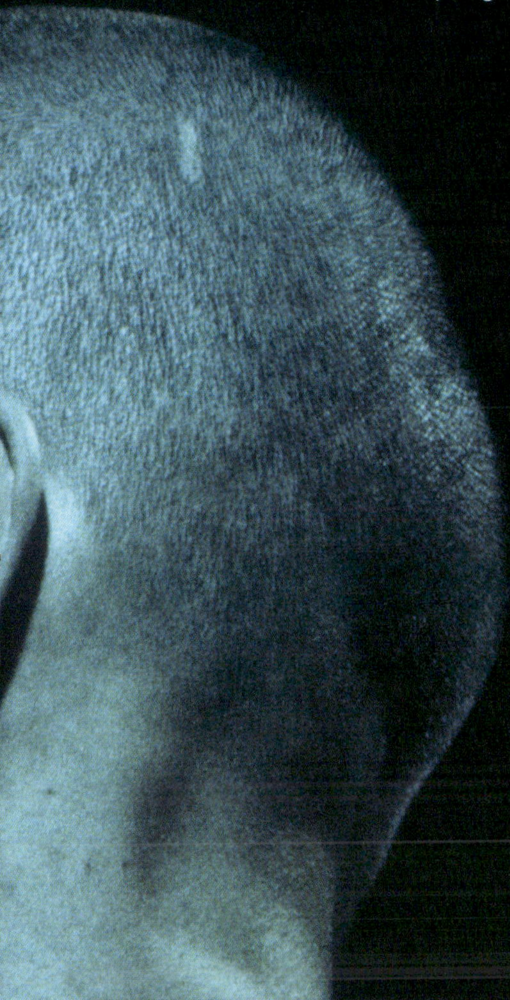

Check out these covers ...

Chris Cornell, punk rock band Me First and the Gimme Gimmes and Stereophonics have all covered the song in their own inimitable styles.

Prince performed *Nothing Compares 2 U* live several times throughout his career and one notable live version recorded with his band, The New Power Generation, in 1993 was included on his compilation album *The Hits/The B-Sides*.

His own original 1984 studio recording was released by his estate in 2018, two years after his death, offering fans a glimpse of his take on the song.

CHRIS CORNELL

PRINCE

Fun fact

O'Connor won a Grammy Award for Best Alternative Music Performance for her album I Do Not Want What I Haven't Got, but she refused to accept the award, protesting the commercialism of the Grammy Awards.

FIRE AND RAIN
JAMES TAYLOR
1970

41

WRITTEN BY: James Taylor
RECORDED: 1969
PRODUCER: Peter Asher
ENGINEER: Bill Lazerus and Richard Sanford Orshoff
RELEASED: February 1970

James Taylor was one of the first successful, soul-baring singer-songwriters of the early '70s and this deeply personal song reflects his struggles with depression, addiction and loss.

The lyrics recount three particular periods of his life – even though he was aged just 21 at the time. The first verse is about his reaction to the suicide of his childhood friend Susie Schnerr, referred to as Suzanne. He then goes on to details his time in a psychiatric hospital dealing with depression and his battles with heroin addiction. A reference to a broken 'flying machine' is often wrongly taken to be about a plane crash, whereas it actually refers to the disbandment of his group Flying Machine, which he'd set up in the mid-1960s.

The 'fire' in the song represents Taylor's shock and anger, while the 'rain' symbolises his sadness and sorrow. The song also touches on the disillusionment of failed dreams and the search for meaning and comfort during challenging times.

Fire and Rain was his breakthrough hit and received widespread acclaim for its emotional depth and Taylor's poignant delivery. Featured on Taylor's second album, *Sweet Baby James*, which was also released in 1970, it was released as a single in February 1970, and reached #3 on the US Billboard chart.

Fun fact

The piano part on Fire and Rain was played by Carole King, James Taylor's great friend and longtime musical collaborator, who also had a noteworthy influence on the singer-songwriter movement.

Check out these covers ...

Fire and Rain has been covered – a lot! With a melody that's so easy on the ear it became a favourite with old school crooners like Jack Jones and Andy Williams, despite its lyrics telling of harrowing despair. The Isley Brothers produced a very cool reinterpretation, while, staying closer to the original, John Denver's version brings a country-inflected interpretation to the song, and Johnny Cash used his deep and emotive voice to add a layer of gravitas to the song's already profound lyrics.

ANDY WILLIAMS

JACK JONES

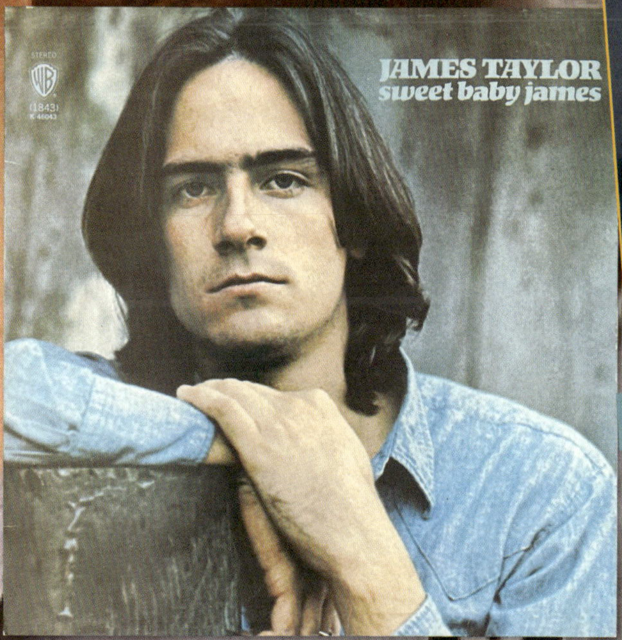

JOHN DENVER

THE ISLEY BROTHERS

LOSING MY RELIGION

R.E.M.

1991

40

WRITTEN BY: Michael Stipe, Peter Buck

RECORDED: September/October 1990

PRODUCER: Scott Litt

ENGINEER: Scott Litt

RELEASED: 19 February 1991

This track manoeuvred R.E.M. from cult indie rockers to international superstardom in 1991 when it was released as the lead single from their seventh studio album *Out Of Time.*

Guitarist Peter Ruck came up with this song's famous riff when learning to play the mandolin. When he listened back to recordings of his first attempts he thought he had the makings of a good song, although with a mandolin as lead instrument and no proper chorus, no one was optimistic for a hit. However, it turned out to be their biggest ever single, peaking at #4 on the Billboard Hot 100 chart and going on to be certified Gold by the Recording Industry Association of America (RIAA) for sales exceeding 500,000 copies. In the UK, the song reached #19 on the UK Singles Chart.

The song is not, of course, about religion but is based on a colloquial phrase, popular in several southern American states, used to explain someone being at the end of their tether or frustrated beyond all reason.

It remains one of the band's most memorable songs, which solidified their status as one of the leading alternative rock bands of the era – versatile and able to connect with audiences on an emotional level.

Check out these covers ...

Among the artists who have paid homage to R.E.M.'s classic track through their own interpretations is Tori Amos, who presented a version using her signature piano-driven sound on her 2001 album *Strange Little Girls.*

The German band Gregorian, known for their Gregorian chant-style covers of popular songs, included a rendition of Losing My Religion on their 2004 album *The Dark Side.*

English singer-songwriter Passenger included a stripped-down acoustic cover of the song as a bonus track on the deluxe edition of his 2016 album *Young as the Morning Old as the Sea.*

TORI AMOS

PASSENGER

GREGORIAN

HEY JUDE
THE BEATLES

1968

39

WRITTEN BY: John Lennon and Paul McCartney

RECORDED: 31 July – 1 August 1968

PRODUCER: George Martin

ENGINEER: Geoff Emerick

RELEASED: 26 August 1968 (US) and 30 August 1968 (UK)

Although credited to Lennon–McCartney, as was customary for their songwriting partnership, McCartney actually wrote this comforting and uplifting anthem by himself, to console John Lennon's son, Julian, during his parents' divorce. Its lyrics offer words of encouragement and support during tough times.

It is reported that McCartney originally intended to title the song 'Hey Jules,' addressing Julian Lennon directly in the lyrics. However, he later changed it to 'Jude' because he thought it sounded better.

At over seven minutes long, *Hey Jude* was one of the longest singles ever released at the time. Its famous extended fade-out, featuring repeated chants of 'na-na-na-na', with improvised shrieks, yelps and handclaps, initially met with scepticism by some in the music industry, who doubted its commercial

greater flexibility in the mixing process and, along with the orchestral accompaniment, contributed to the song's rich and dynamic sound.

It topped the charts in multiple countries and became the band's biggest-selling single in the United States, spending nine consecutive weeks at #1 on the Billboard Hot 100 and a total of 19 weeks on the chart overall. It also topped the charts around the world and was the best-selling single for that year in Canada, Australia and the UK.

The song is also notable for being one of four songs, released simultaneously, to launch The Beatles' Apple record label. Together with *MacArthur Park* (which had been a hit, one second shorter, that same year) *Hey Jude* also paved the way for other 'long songs' such as *Layla* and *American Pie*. DJs came to like the fact they could take a break while those long records played out.

Check out these covers ...

Various artists have paid homage to *Hey Jude* with their own versions, including Wilson Pickett and Elvis Presley.

ELVIS PRESLEY

WILSON PICKETT

NIGHTS IN WHITE SATIN
MOODY BLUES
1967

38

WRITTEN BY: Justin Haywood
RECORDED: 8 October 1967
PRODUCER: Tony Clarke
ENGINEER: Derek Varnals
RELEASED: 3 November 1967 (UK), January 1968 (US)

***Nights in White Satin* is a melancholic ballad reflecting themes of unrequited love, longing and the passage of time. It was the final track on the band's concept album *Days of Future Passed,* with the tracks all based around different times of day.**

The lyrics, written by band member Justin Hayward when he was just 19, set out to capture the emotional turmoil and introspection of a young man dealing with the complexities of love. He was said to have been inspired to write the song quite literally after receiving a gift of satin bedsheets.

Musically, the song features rich orchestral arrangements and the distinctive sound of the Mellotron, an early keyboard instrument that produces orchestral sounds. Its ethereal melody, coupled with Hayward's emotive vocals combines with the orchestration to create the dreamy, atmospheric quality that has become a hallmark of the song.

A six-minute long song was unusual in those times and on its initial release, *Nights in White Satin* charted modestly, reaching #19 in the UK and #103 in the US. However, when re-released in 1972, it achieved greater success, reaching

#2 on the Billboard Hot 100 and #9 in the UK. This is possibly because longer songs had become more commercially viable following the success of lengthy tracks like *Hey Jude* and *Layla*. In the UK, the song charted once more, in 1979, to reach #14.

Check out these covers ...

Eric Burdon & The Animals paid tribute to the Moody Blues with their version adding a more soulful rock interpretation.

Then in the 1980s the German pop singer Sandra brought the song to a new audience.

The operatic pop group Il Divo gave their version, ***Notte di Luce***, a classical crossover twist.

However, Justin Hayward once said that the 2013 version by soul singer Bettye LaVette was his favourite.

BETTYE LAVETTE

SANDRA

PURPLE HAZE
JIMI HENDRIX EXPERIENCE
1967

37

WRITTEN BY: Jimi Hendrix

RECORDED: 11 January and 3 February 1967

PRODUCER: Chas Chandler

ENGINEER: Eddie Kramer

RELEASED: 17 March 1967 (UK) and 19 June 1967 (US)

One of Jimi Hendrix's signature songs and a quintessential track of the psychedelic rock era, *Purple Haze* is known for its innovative guitar riffs, heavy use of distortion and Hendrix's unique playing style, which set a new standard for rock music.

The opening guitar riff is one of the most recognisable in rock history, and brilliantly showcases Hendrix's virtuosic technique and creativity. The distinctive and bluesy 'Hendrix chord' he developed (a dominant E7#9 chord) and his use of feedback, distortion and the wah-wah pedal, showcased his groundbreaking approach to guitar playing.

The studio recording similarly featured pioneering studio techniques such as tape echo and reverse tape effects to create the song's unique soundscapes, contributing to the psychedelic feel which went on to influence countless musicians.

It is often interpreted as a song that blends psychedelic rock with surreal imagery, reflecting the era's countercultural movement. The lyrics are famously ambiguous, often thought to refer to an altered state of consciousness, which some interpret as a reference to drugs. But Hendrix himself denied that it was specifically about drug use and instead mentioned that it was inspired by a vivid dream he had and also the science fiction stories he enjoyed.

Purple Haze reached #3 on the UK Singles Chart and #65 on the Billboard Hot 100 in the US. It wasn't his first single but was the one which people most connect with him and made him and his backing band the 'Experience' more famous. Hendrix and the Experience frequently performed it live, often improvising and extending the song during concerts. He was a dynamic and unpredictable performer, most notably evidenced at the Monterey Pop Festival in 1967, when he famously set his guitar on fire.

Check out these covers ...

Many acts have covered *Purple Haze,* including The Cure who added a post-punk twist and Frank Zappa who included his signature complex and avant-garde style.

THE CURE

FRANK ZAPPA

Jimi Hendrix Experience, 1968

STAIRWAY TO HEAVEN

LED ZEPPELIN

1971

36

WRITTEN BY: Jimmy Page and Robert Plant

RECORDED: December 1970 – March 1971

PRODUCER: Jimmy Page

ENGINEER: Andy Johns

RELEASED: 8 November 1971

S*tairway to Heaven* explores themes of spiritual discovery and enlightenment. The lyrics, written by Robert Plant, begin with the story of a woman who is 'buying' said stairway, but as the song progresses, it delves into deeper philosophical and existential themes. The song's structure reflects this journey, starting with a slow, acoustic intro and gradually building to a powerful, electrifying climax.

Renowned for this complex structure, multi-layered with an intricate musical arrangement, it is frequently listed among the greatest rock songs of all time.

Musically it transitions through multiple styles, starting with a folk-inspired acoustic guitar introduction, before moving into rock, and finally culminating in a hard rock section with an outstanding guitar solo by Jimmy Page which is considered one of the greatest in rock history.

released as a single in the UK or the US, *Stairway to Heaven* became one of the most requested and played songs on FM radio stations in the 1970s. It set the standard by which other rock anthems are assessed.

Lauded by critics and fans alike for its lyrical depth, innovative structure and masterful musicianship, the song has had a profound impact on rock music and popular culture.

Check out these covers ...

Dolly Parton added an Americana feel to the song when she included it on her 2002 album, *Halos & Horns* including banjo, fiddle, acoustic guitar, a choir and revised lyrics.

Frank Zappa, known for his eclectic style, produced a cover which is both a tribute and a reimagining.

Another definitive performance, which received widespread acclaim, came when the American, female-fronted rock band Heart gave a live performance at the Kennedy Center Honors in 2012 when Led Zeppelin were honoured by President Barack Obama for their contribution to American culture.

FRANK ZAPPA

DOLLY PARTON

HEART

THE FIRST TIME EVER I SAW YOUR FACE

ROBERTA FLACK

1969

35

WRITTEN BY: Ewan MacColl

RECORDED: 1969

PRODUCER: Joel Dorn

ENGINEER: Gene Paul

RELEASED: 20 June 1969

This soulful love song was written by British folk musician Ewan MacColl in 1957 for his future wife, fellow folk star Peggy Seeger. It was his description of the deep emotions he'd experienced upon seeing her for the first time, with lyrics conveying the profound sense of love, intimacy and the transformative power of that first encounter.

'I wish more songs I had chosen had moved me the way that one did,' said Roberta of the track, which first appeared on her album *First Take*. 'I've loved [most] every song I've recorded, but that one (*The First Time Ever I Saw Your Face*) was pretty special'.

Her version of the song became a major hit after it was featured in the 1971 film 'Play Misty for Me'. It reached #1 on the Billboard Hot 100 and stayed there for six weeks in 1972. The single topped the Easy Listening chart for six weeks and was certified gold. It also won that year's Grammy Awards for Record of the Year and Song of the Year.

Roberta Flack's emotionally intense, powerful yet understated vocal performance established her as a major star, and the song has remained one of her signature songs.

Check out these covers ...

Widely recognised as one of the greatest love songs of all time, the song continues to be a popular choice for reinterpretation, with some truly great artists adding it to their repertoire.

Elvis Presley added a distinctively smooth vibe to his version of the classic, while Johnny Cash's cover offered a more country-tinged interpretation.

Two powerhouse female singers, Celine Dion and Leona Lewis, each showcased their powerful vocal range and emotional delivery when they sang the song and George Michael's heartfelt rendition on his album *Songs from the Last Century* stayed completely true to the song's original emotion.

CELINE DION

GEORGE MICHAEL

YOU DON'T HAVE TO SAY YOU LOVE ME

DUSTY SPRINGFIELD

1966

34

WRITTEN BY: Pino Donaggio, Vito Pallavicini
UK Lyrics by Vicki Wickham and Simon Napier-Bell

RECORDED: Early 1966

PRODUCER: Johnny Franz

ENGINEER: Uncredited

RELEASED: March 1966

This soulful ballad gave Dusty Springfield her biggest hit – a UK #1 and a top 4 on the US Billboard chart.

Hailed at the time as the British Queen of Soul, Dusty's signature vocal style was once described by Bette Midler as 'haunting and husky... full of secrets and promises'. She'd been a successful solo artist for three years – but never had a #1 until she released this track which was a cover of an Italian song *Io che non vivo (senza te)*. With new English lyrics, delivered so powerfully and emotionally, Dusty crafted a huge international hit by blending her love of soul with this European pop song.

The story goes that she achieved the desired echo on her voice by moving out of the recording studio into the stairwell and singing into a microphone suspended halfway up the stairs.

Check out these covers …

As one of the most emotionally resonant songs of the 1960s, *You Don't Have to Say You Love Me* has inspired numerous covers and adaptations across genres. The best is Elvis Presley's 1970 soulful version which became the second single from his album *That's the Way It Is*. This went to #11 on the US Billboard Hot 100 and #1 on its Easy Listening listing, as well as charting in the UK, Ireland, elsewhere in Europe, Australia and Canada. It was also a huge hit in Japan where it made Elvis the first foreign artist to have the best-selling record of the year in 1971. Cher also covered the song on her 1966 self-titled album.

ELVIS PRESLEY

CHER

RIVER DEEP – MOUNTAIN HIGH
IKE AND TINA TURNER

1966

33

WRITTEN BY: Phil Spector, Jeff Barry and Ellie Greenwich

RECORDED: Early 1966

PRODUCER: Phil Spector

ENGINEER: Studio engineer (uncredited)

RELEASED: May 1966

The successful husband and wife songwriting team of Barry and Greenwich had a string of hits to their name, including 1964's *Leader of the Pack* and *Do Wah Diddy Diddy*, before writing the classic *River Deep - Mountain High* together with legendary producer Spector, famous for his Wall of Sound production technique. Reportedly all three writers came to the session with separate, unfinished songs, which they then combined.

Musically the song is characterised by its sweeping orchestral arrangement, featuring lush strings and driving percussion to make a richly layered sonic tapestry that perfectly complemented Tina Turner's electrifying performance. Spector particularly wanted Tina to record the song, knowing that her incendiary vocals could cut through the dense production he wanted to create.

All their talents came together to create a sense of grandeur and drama that is both captivating and unforgettable.

The recording process, which was groundbreaking at the time, cost US$22,000 – equivalent to $207,000 today and an unheard of price tag in the 1960s.

To Spector's dismay, the song didn't do well in America, where he was keen to have a hit record after many months without one. But *River Deep, Mountain High* was a big hit in the UK, where it went to #3.

Check out these covers ...

Many other versions of *River Deep - Mountain High* been recorded, including covers by Eric Burden and The Animals, on their 1968 album *Love Is*, and Neil Diamond a year later.

Perhaps the most surprising reinterpretation of them all was by hard rock band Deep Purple who gave the song an innovative spin for their second studio album, *The Book of Taliesyn,* released in 1968.

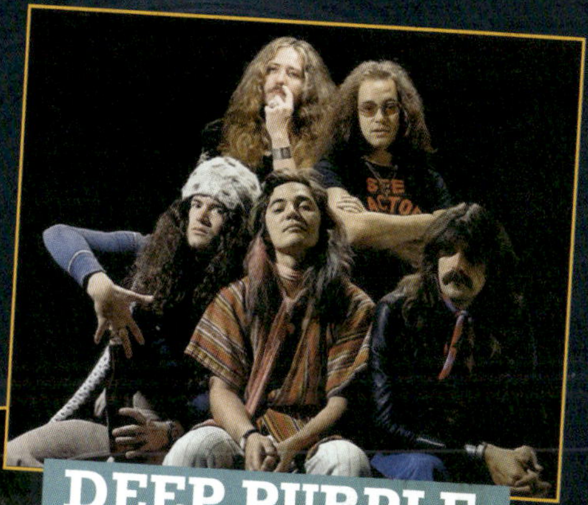

DEEP PURPLE

ERIC BURDEN AND THE ANIMALS

NEIL DIAMOND

Fun fact

Although the song was credited to Ike and Tina Turner, Tina's husband Ike had no part in it.

FOLSOM PRISON BLUES

JOHNNY CASH

1955

32

WRITTEN BY: Johnny Cash

RECORDED: 30 July 1955

PRODUCER: Sam Phillips

ENGINEER: Bill Porter

RELEASED: 15 December 1955

This song, which came to define Johnny Cash's professional persona, was first released as a single in 1955, then included two years later on his debut studio album *Johnny Cash with His Hot and Blue Guitar!*

Combining elements of country, rockabilly and blues, the song was reportedly inspired by the 1951 film 'Inside the Walls of Folsom Prison'. Cash added his own dramatic flair to the lyrics in a first-person narrative sung from the perspective of an inmate at Folsom Prison who laments his fate and yearns for freedom. The song's most famous line about shooting a man 'just to watch him die', vividly captures the remorse and hopelessness of the character.

The song features a distinctive train-like rhythm, which complements its themes of confinement and longing. Cash's deep, resonant voice, combined with his minimalistic guitar playing and the steady beat provided by his backing band, the Tennessee Two, creates a haunting and memorable sound.

The original recording was a hit on the country music charts, peaking at #4. Then when a more up tempo version was recorded live at concert inside Folsom Prison itself in January 1968, in front of an audience of inmates, the performance added a layer of realism and connection to the song's narrative. Cash's career was revitalised as his song reached #1 on the country charts and #32 on the Billboard Hot 100 that summer.

Check out these covers ...

While many covers, such as those from Merle Haggard and Brooks & Dunn, retained the song's country feel, a few artists have tried an original approach, including Jerry Lee Lewis, known for his rock and roll and rockabilly style, who added an energetic twist to the classic. More recently, American rapper Everlast introduced a modern, bluesy feel to the song, appealing to contemporary audiences.

JERRY LEE LEWIS

EVERLAST

MERLE HAGGARD

LONDON CALLING
THE CLASH
1980

31

WRITTEN BY: Joe Strummer and Mick Jones

RECORDED: August/September 1979

PRODUCER: Guy Stevens

ENGINEER: Bill Price

RELEASED: 7 December 1979 (UK); January 1980 (US)

L*ondon Calling* is a powerful song addressing the social and political issues prevalent in the late 1970s. The lyrics are a response to the anxiety and unease of the time, touching on nuclear power, environmental issues, police brutality and youthful disillusionment. The phrase 'London Calling' is a reference to BBC World Service radio broadcasts during World War II, which began with the words 'This is London calling'.

Reflecting a sense of urgency and rebellion, it captured the mood of a generation grappling with economic instability and political unrest. It also alludes to the band's fear of an uncertain future, with mentions of nuclear error.

Musically the song features a distinctive blend of punk rock, reggae and rockabilly influences, all driven by a strong bassline and a rhythmic guitar riff, beneath Joe Strummer's impassioned vocals. It has one of the most recognisable and stirring intros in rock. The production retains the raw energy for which The Clash was famous, while maintaining a polished, propulsive sound that helped broaden their appeal.

It reached #11 on the UK Singles Chart and #30 on the US Billboard Mainstream Rock chart. The album of the same name, the band's third, is often cited as one of the greatest of all time and its cover is similarly revered as a pop culture icon. It was a homage to one of the first rock and roll records ever, the self-titled debut album by Elvis Presley but with a photo of Clash bassist Paul Simonon crashing his guitar on stage.

Check out these covers ...

Bruce Springsteen has performed the song live on many occasions, adding his own rock influence, most notably at his London Hyde Park set in 2009.

The Pogues also performed the track, with Joe Strummer, on their *Live in London* album.

BRUCE SPRINGSTEEN

THE POGUES

REDEMPTION SONG

BOB MARLEY

1980

30

WRITTEN BY: Bob Marley

RECORDED: 1980

PRODUCER: Chris Blackwell

ENGINEER: Chiao Ng and Errol Brown

RELEASED: October 1980

R*edemption Song* is widely considered to be one of Bob Marley's greatest songs, despite it sounding quite unlike most of his other recordings. With none of his trademark reggae rhythm and without his Wailers backing band, Bob Marley gives a simple acoustic performance, accompanying himself on guitar. This stark presentation helps to highlight the raw and poignant nature of its themes of personal freedom, social justice and human rights.

Serving as a powerful anthem for freedom and liberation, the lyrics were inspired by a speech given by the prominent Jamaican political leader and activist, Marcus Garvey, in which he emphasised self-emancipation.

It was recorded as the final track on Marley's *Uprising* album and was first performed at the opening show of the album's accompanying tour on 30 May 1980, in Switzerland, and at many of the shows afterwards.

At that time Marley was suffering from cancer and many people believe they can hear a 'farewell' in the song. He died in May 1981 and certainly his illness would have coloured his work in those final years. As one of his last recordings, it holds a special place in his discography, encapsulating his life-long advocacy for justice and equality. The song's simplicity and profound lyrics ensure that it will continue to be a rallying cry for those seeking freedom and redemption.

Check out these covers ...

The ballad has been covered many times including versions by Joe Strummer of The Clash, both with The Mescaleros and with Johnny Cash, and Chris Cornell. Rihanna and Leon Bridges have also sung the song, bringing it to modern audiences.

JOE STRUMMER

RIHANNA

JOHNNY CASH

LEON BRIDGES

STAND BY ME
BEN E. KING
1961

29

WRITTEN BY: Ben E. King, Gerry Lieber and Mike Stoller
RECORDED: March 1961
PRODUCER: Leiber and Stoller
ENGINEER: (uncredited)
RELEASED: April 1961

Beyond its chart success, *Stand By Me* has become a cultural touchstone that has had a profound impact on popular culture through its timeless message of loyalty, camaraderie and support.

Inspired by a hymn that drew inspiration from a psalm, the song has echoes of gospel music and is thought to have originated in the early 1900s as song first published by Methodist minister and composer Charles Albert Tindley, son of a slave. However, its origins may extend even further back into the black American oral tradition.

Updated by Ben E. King, with a Brazilian-inspired rhythm added by Leiber and Stoller, the song enjoyed immediate success in the US charts where it soared to #1 on the Billboard R&B Chart and #4 on the Billboard Hot 100, catapulting King to fame following his departure from The Drifters.

Solidifying his status as a soul music icon, King's soulful vocals combined with the song's simple yet powerful lyrics and the famous bassline, to strike a chord with listeners and become a covert protest song, with a well-deserved place in the pantheon of classics.

Check out these covers ...

One of the most remarkable aspects of *Stand By Me* is its enduring legacy. Over the years, the song has been covered by hundreds of artists from various genres, including John Lennon, Otis Redding and Tracy Chapman.

The song has been featured prominently in numerous films, television shows and commercials as an anthem of love and friendship. It was also sung by The Kingdom Choir during the royal wedding of Prince Harry and Meghan Markle at St George's Chapel, Windsor in 2018.

OTIS REDDING

TRACY CHAPMAN

JOHN LENNON

BOTH SIDES NOW
JONI MITCHELL
1969

28

WRITTEN BY: Joni Mitchell
RECORDED: 1969
PRODUCER: Joni Mitchell
ENGINEER: Henry Lewy
RELEASED: 1969

Praised for its lyrical depth and emotional resonance, *Both Sides Now* is considered a classic of the folk genre.

From her album *Clouds*, it became one of Canadian singer-songwriter Joni Mitchell's best-known songs. It is a contemplative piece, reflecting on the dualities and complexities of life and love, viewed from different perspectives over time. The lyrics explore the idea of seeing things from both sides – the idealistic, naive view and the more experienced, disillusioned perspective. Joni Mitchell reportedly wrote it on a plane having been inspired by her view out of the window at the clouds beneath her and using them as a metaphor to convey the shifts in understanding and perception as one grows older. Her original version is characterised by her distinct folk style, with acoustic guitar and subtle orchestration.

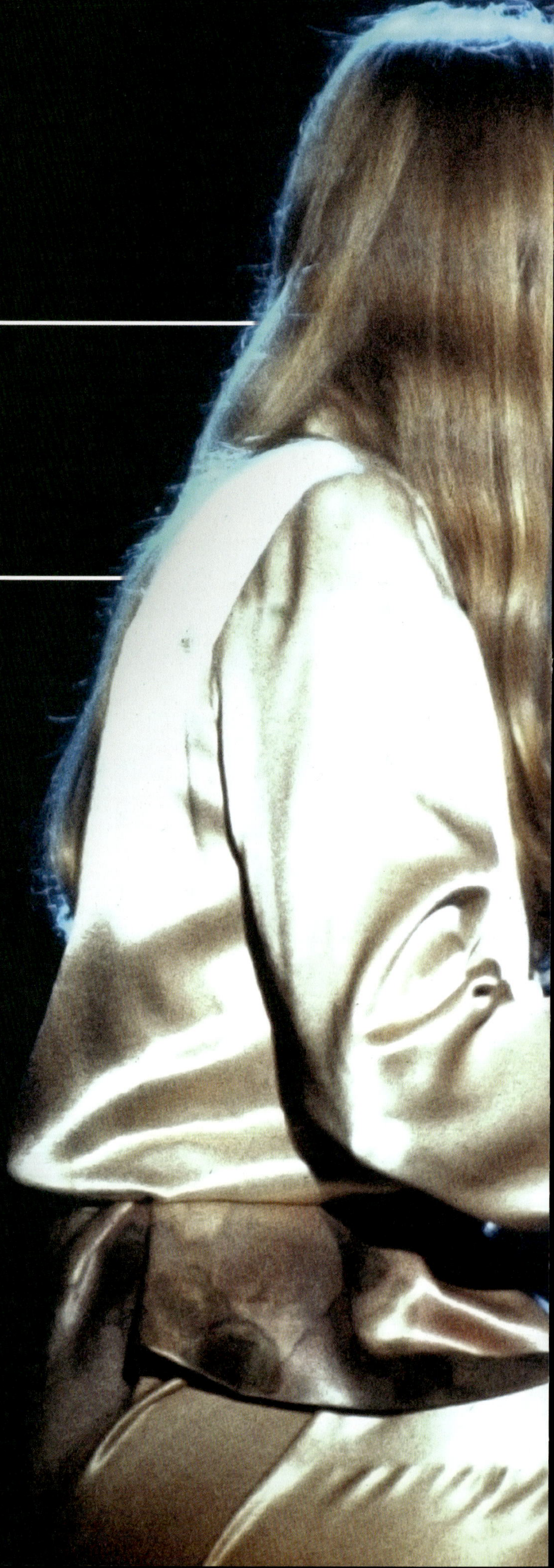

Check out these covers ...

Before Joni Mitchell released her version, Judy Collins had the first commercially successful hit with the song in October 1967. It was a major hit, reaching #8 on the Billboard Hot 100 and helping to bring Joni Mitchell's songwriting to a broader audience. Other artists who have covered it include Frank Sinatra and Neil Diamond.

Joni Mitchell re-recorded the song herself for her 2000 album *Both Sides Now*, featuring a more mature, jazz-influenced arrangement.

JUDY COLLINS

NEIL DIAMOND

WHAT'D I SAY

RAY CHARLES

1959

27

WRITTEN BY: Ray Charles
RECORDED: February 1959
PRODUCER: Jerry Wexler
ENGINEER: Tom Dowd
RELEASED: July 1959

What'd I Say is a landmark recording and one of the first 'soul' songs. Its groundbreaking fusion of musical styles, coupled with an exuberant, spontaneous energy, captured the spirit of a transformative era in American music.

The song was a huge cross-over hit for Ray Charles, becoming his first gold record, selling over a million copies, peaking at #1 on the Billboard R&B chart and #6 on the Billboard Hot 100. This mainstream success not only solidified his reputation as a pioneering artist, but also helped to shape the future of popular music by bridging the gap between R&B and rock and roll.

It's an electrifying rhythm and blues song that captures the spontaneous energy of Ray Charles's live performances, having originated accidentally during a live show when Charles, having run out of material to play, improvised the piece on the spot. It is built around a catchy riff, playful call-and-response vocals and a propulsive beat that fuses gospel, blues and jazz elements. The song's suggestive lyrics and exuberant performance made it both a hit and a subject of controversy due to its perceived sexual innuendos.

The song is divided into two parts: the first half features a driving piano riff and Charles's powerful vocals, while the second half shifts to a more gospel-influenced call-and-response section between Charles and his backup singers, The Raelettes. The use of Latin-influenced rhythms, particularly the mambo beat, adds to the song's infectious energy.

The Raelettes

Check out these covers ...

The song's upbeat tempo, innovative use of electric piano and blend of different musical styles influenced a generation of musicians, including The Beatles and The Rolling Stones who performed the song during their early years.

Elvis Presley performed the song in a dance scene for his 1964 film *Viva Las Vegas* and it was also the B-side of the film's title song. Jerry Lee Lewis was successful with his 1961 rockabilly version in 1961, which peaked at #30 and spent eight weeks on the Billboard charts. Bobby Darin, Cliff Richard, Nancy Sinatra and even Eric Clapton are among a long list of artists who have also put their spin on the song.

THE ROLLING STONES

ERIC CLAPTON

SMELLS LIKE TEEN SPIRIT

NIRVANA

1991

26

WRITTEN BY: Kurt Cobain, Krist Novoselic and Dave Grohl

RECORDED: May 1991

PRODUCER: Butch Vig

ENGINEER: Butch Vig

RELEASED: 10 September 1991

S*mells Like Teen Spirit* remains one of the most influential songs in rock history. It not only defined the career of American rock band Nirvana but also became a defining anthem of the 1990s, helping to pave the way for mainstream acceptance of alternative rock and grunge.

Released as the lead single from Nirvana's second album, *Nevermind*, it peaked at #6 on the Billboard Hot 100 and topped the charts in several countries. Its massive commercial success helped propel *Nevermind* to the #1 spot on the Billboard 200.

As a symbol of youthful rebellion it captured the zeitgeist of an era full of angst, apathy and disillusionment. The song's lyrics are famously cryptic and have been interpreted in various ways. Kurt Cobain, who wrote the song, claimed it was his attempt to write a pop song in the style of the Pixies. His fellow band members Novoselic and Grohl weren't keen on the track at first, but after adding their spin on bass and drums respectively, the song went on to be credited to the whole band.

The song features a dynamic, loud-quiet-loud structure, heavily distorted guitars and Cobain's raw, gritty vocals. It opens with a distinctive four-chord guitar riff played by Cobain, followed by the explosive entrance of the rhythm section, with powerful drumming and a driving bassline. The verses are relatively subdued, creating a stark contrast with the explosive choruses

Fun fact – the title came from a piece of graffiti left on Cobain's wall by Kathleen Hanna of the band Bikini Kill, which read 'Kurt smells like Teen Spirit' – a reference to a brand of deodorant, which Cobain later said he initially did not realise.

Check out these covers ...

Having inspired countless musicians and bands, stand out covers include the haunting, piano-based version from Tori Amos, which strips the song down to its emotional core, offering a stark contrast to the original's intensity.

The punk rock icon Patti Smith added her own poetic verses to the song, creating a unique and personal rendition. Then jazz singer Paul Anka's swing version further showcased the song's versatility, while probably horrifying Generation X devotees of the original.

Most recently Malia J's slow and brooding cover, featured in the opening credits of the 2021 film *Black Widow*.

PATTI SMITH

PAUL ANKA

Dave Grohl, Kurt Cobain & Krist Novoselic

LOVE WILL TEAR US APART

JOY DIVISION

1980

25

WRITTEN BY: Ian Curtis, Bernard Sumner, Peter Hook and Stephen Morris

RECORDED: November 1979 and January 1980

PRODUCER: Martin Hannett

ENGINEER: John Caffery

RELEASED: 27 June 1980

L*ove Will Tear Us Apart* has become an anthem of the post-punk movement and a symbol of Joy Division's tragic legacy as it was released just a month after the death of lead singer Ian Curtis. The band's most successful track – reaching #13 on the UK Singles Chart – it is an exploration of personal pain and emotional conflict which resonated deeply with listeners and influenced artists across various genres.

Delving into themes of love, disillusionment and emotional turmoil, the lyrics written by Ian Curtis reflect his personal struggles, particularly the breakdown of his marriage and his battle with depression and epilepsy.

The song features a distinctive and melancholic melody, driven by Peter Hook's boss bassline and Bernard Sumner's shimmering guitar work. The production adds a haunting, atmospheric quality with its use of reverb and echo. Curtis's baritone vocals, combined with the song's upbeat tempo and bleak lyrics, create a striking contrast that has contributed to the song's continuing success.

Check out these covers …

The 1983 version by Paul Young reached #9 on the UK Singles Chart and introduced the song to a wider audience.

The Scottish band Simple Minds included their rendition as a bonus track on their 2001 album *Neon Lights – Deluxe Edition*, and the American rock band Fall Out Boy, added a contemporary pop-punk twist to their cover of the song in 2008.

PAUL YOUNG

SIMPLE MINDS

FALL OUT BOY

RESPECT
ARETHA FRANKLIN
1967

24

WRITTEN BY: Otis Redding
RECORDED: February 1967
PRODUCER: Jerry Wexler
ENGINEER: Tom Dowd
RELEASED: April 1967

This is a great example of a cover outdoing an original. First written and released by the renowned soul singer and songwriter Otis Reading in 1965, the song was propelled to even greater heights when it was covered by 'Queen of Soul' Aretha Franklin two years later on her 1967 album *I Never Loved a Man the Way I Love You.*

Aretha's version reimagined the song with a more assertive and empowering message, transforming it into an anthem for empowerment and equality. Its new lyrics and sound transformed the song so that it became a rallying cry for the civil rights and feminist movements which were re-shaping America's cultural landscape.

At the song's heart is its catchy rhythm and soulful energy, driven by Franklin's powerhouse vocals, backed by a dynamic arrangement of horns, drums and backing vocals.

Lyrically, *Respect* delivers a potent message of self-worth as Aretha sets out the demands for respect and recognition she deserves in her personal relationships. Yet Aretha's rearrangement completely developed the song, making it a call to action that seared into the public consciousness. She also added the memorable chorus, with the repeated refrain of 'R-E-S-P-E-C-T,' and the 'sock it to me' chant, both of which make the song so instantly recognisable.

Respect was a massive chart success, reaching #1 on the Billboard Hot 100 chart in the United States where it remained for 12 weeks, becoming one of Aretha Franklin's signature songs.

Check out these covers ...

While no other artist has repeated the chart success enjoyed by Aretha Franklin's version, many artists have sung the song, which has also featured in numerous films including *Forrest Gump* and *Bridget Jones's Diary*, as well as being used in political campaigns. It has moved beyond the pop music world to become an anthem for all those who feel they have been taken for granted or disempowered in love, business and life.

American band Train released a cover of *Respect* as a single in 2010, which reached the top 100 on the Billboard Hot 100 chart. Diana Ross has covered *Respect* during some of her live performances, as have The Supremes, although neither artist's versions charted as hit singles.

In fact, the most recent performance to make an impact was the impassioned rendition from Aretha herself at the 1998 Grammy Awards, when she sang alongside The Blues Brothers.

TRAIN

CANDLE IN THE WIND
ELTON JOHN
1974/1997

23

WRITTEN BY: Elton John and Bernie Taupin

RECORDED: 1973, then again between 7–11 September 1997

PRODUCER: Gus Dudgeon, then George Martin for 1997

ENGINEER: David Hentschel, then an uncredited studio engineer for 1997

RELEASED: 7 April 1974, then 13 September 1997

Originally written for Elton's 1973 album *Goodbye Yellow Brick Road*, the track *Candle in the Wind* was a tribute to the actress Marilyn Monroe and is, more generally, about the idea of fame and youth and somebody's life being cut short in their prime. In 1974 when it was first released as a single it reached #11 in the British charts.

However the song had a second life when it was later re-written and re-released in 1997 as a tribute to Diana, Princess of Wales following her tragic death. Elton John, who was a friend of the Princess, performed the moving lament at her funeral in Westminster Abbey on 6 September 1997.

The 1997 version, titled *Candle in the Wind 1997*, and also known by its first line *Goodbye England's Rose*, went on to become one of the best-selling singles of all time, with estimated sales exceeding 33 million copies worldwide.

A fantastic marriage of lyrics and melody, it topped the charts in numerous countries, including the United Kingdom and the United States, where it spent 14 weeks at #1 on the Billboard Hot 100 chart.

Although he has subsequently sung the original version of the song at his concerts, Elton has never since performed the 1997 version, having vowed not to do so unless asked by Diana's sons the Princes William and Harry.

A live version of the original song, recorded in Sydney, Australia in 1986, earned Elton John a Grammy Award for Best Male Pop Vocal Performance in 1988. The track remains one of his most beloved songs.

Check out these covers …

Ed Sheeran sang the original version for the 2018 album *Reimagining the Songs of Elton John and Bernie Taupin.*

ED SHEERAN

WHAT'S GOING ON
MARVIN GAYE

1971

22

WRITTEN BY: Marvin Gaye, Al Cleveland and Renaldo "Obie" Benson

RECORDED: 1 June 1970

PRODUCER: Marvin Gaye

ENGINEER: Ken Sands and Steve Smith

RELEASED: 17 January 1971

What's Going On **is a soulful plea for peace and understanding amidst the social turmoil and unrest of the late 1960s and early 1970s. The song was inspired by Renaldo "Obie" Benson of the Four Tops, who witnessed police brutality at anti-war protests in Berkeley, California. The lyrics reflect Gaye's personal anguish over issues such as the Vietnam War, police brutality and the general social injustices affecting the United States at that time.**

The song is notable for its conversational tone, with Gaye expressing concern and confusion over the state of the world and highlighting the need for compassion and understanding. Musically it features a smooth, jazz-influenced arrangement with lush strings, a prominent bassline and a groove that blends elements of soul, jazz and gospel. Gaye's multi-tracked vocals create a layered and harmonious sound, adding to the song's emotional depth, while the saxophone riff and bassline are especially memorable elements of the arrangement.

The single's huge commercial success, reaching #2 on the Billboard Hot 100 and #1 on the Billboard R&B Singles chart, helped propel the album of the same name to critical and commercial acclaim. This not only solidified Marvin Gaye's legacy as one of the greatest soul artists of all time, but also showcased the potential for pop music to address profound and pressing social issues.

Its success marked Gaye's shift from the traditional Motown Sound to more personal and introspective material. Selling over two million copies, it became Gaye's second-most successful Motown song and the fastest ever selling Motown single of the time.

Check out these covers ...

Cyndi Lauper, Seal and Chaka Khan and the Funk Brothers have all sung the song and in 2001 a star-studded 'pop up' group, including Bono, Destiny's Child and Jennifer Lopez, singing together as Artists Against AIDS Worldwide, sang a cover to raise funds for AIDS research.

CYNDI LAUPER

CHAKA KHAN

SATELLITE OF LOVE

LOU REED

1973

21

WRITTEN BY: Lou Reed

RECORDED: 1970 (original demo)

PRODUCER: David Bowie and Mick Ronson

ENGINEER: Uncredited studio engineer

RELEASED: February 1973

This timeless classic by Lou Reed, from his 1972 album *Transformer*, is characterised by its dreamy melody and introspective lyrics.

It has captivated audiences for decades with its emotional depth and haunting beauty as an exploration of themes of longing, isolation and the search for connection in a world filled with loneliness and uncertainty.

Reed's distinctive vocals, were accompanied by lush instrumentation and ethereal background sounds, including additional vocals by David Bowie, creating a sense of yearning and vulnerability. The lyrics also included hints of jealousy and betrayal, adding depth and complexity to the song's narrative. Producers Bowie and Mick Ronson had been huge fans and champions of Lou Reed since his earlier days with the band Velvet Underground.

Satellite of Love received critical acclaim upon its release and has since become one of Lou Reed's most enduring songs. But it was never a big hit in the charts, reaching #119 in the US at the time, while an updated version, titled *Satellite of Love '04* made it to #10 on the UK Singles Chart in 2004.

Check out these covers …

The song's timeless appeal and universal themes have inspired countless covers and adaptations by artists across genres, cementing its status as a classic of the rock and roll canon. Among them, rock superstars U2 covered *Satellite of Love* and used it as a B-side to some EP versions of their 1991 hit single *One*.

U2

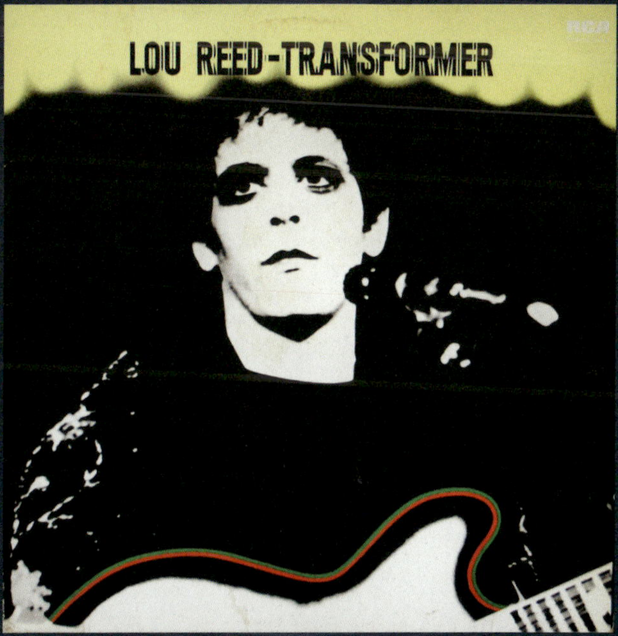

UNCHAINED MELODY
THE RIGHTEOUS BROTHERS

1965

20

WRITTEN BY: Alex North (music) and Hy Zaret (lyrics)

RECORDED: 1965

PRODUCER: Phil Spector

ENGINEER: Bruce Swedien

RELEASED: July 1965

Beloved for its emotional depth and beautiful tune, *Unchained Melody* regularly features in lists of the greatest songs ever recorded.

Originally written for the 1955 prison film *Unchained*, it was immediately covered with three versions making the US Top Ten, and four artists, including Jimmy Young and Liberace, enjoying a UK hit with the song.

But it's the 1965 interpretation by The Righteous Brothers, featuring Bobby Hatfield's exceptional lead vocals, which really took the song to the next level. Their rendition is notable for its dramatic and emotional delivery, with Phil Spector's production adding a lush, orchestral arrangement that complemented the song's intense sentiment. The recording features his renowned 'Wall of Sound' technique, although in a more restrained form compared to other productions.

This soulful version of *Unchained Melody* became a major hit, reaching #4 on the Billboard Hot 100 chart and #14 on the UK Singles Chart. It has since been re-released multiple times, achieving further success with each release.

Poster for the 1955 prison film Unchained

The ballad's enduring popularity was further boosted by its inclusion in the 1990 film *Ghost*, where it was used in the pivotal and memorable 'pottery scene' featuring Patrick Swayze and Demi Moore. With lyrics expressing deep longing, enduring love and a yearning to be reunited with a loved one, the song perfectly captured the pain of separation the characters were feeling.

Check out these covers ...

Over 1,500 recordings of *Unchained Melody* have been made by more than 670 artists, in multiple languages, according to the song's publishing administrator. Of these, The Righteous Brothers' version, in particular, has left a lasting legacy, but key among other renditions, Elvis Presley performed the song live several times, and his cover, notable for its raw emotional intensity, was released posthumously.

The song's versatility is best showcased by the fact that it was been a hit for soul singer Al Green, who put a gospel spin on it, while country music star LeAnn Rimes had a hit on the country charts with her 1997 cover, and U2 have also performed it.

***Unchained Melody* again topped the charts when it became a UK #1 for Gareth Gates, the British singer who was runner-up in the first series of the ITV talent show Pop Idol in 2002.**

LEANN RIMES

AL GREEN

BILLIE JEAN

MICHAEL JACKSON

1983

19

WRITTEN BY: Michael Jackson

RECORDED: April to November 1982

PRODUCER: Michael Jackson and Quincy Jones

ENGINEER: Bruce Swedien

RELEASED: 3 January 1983

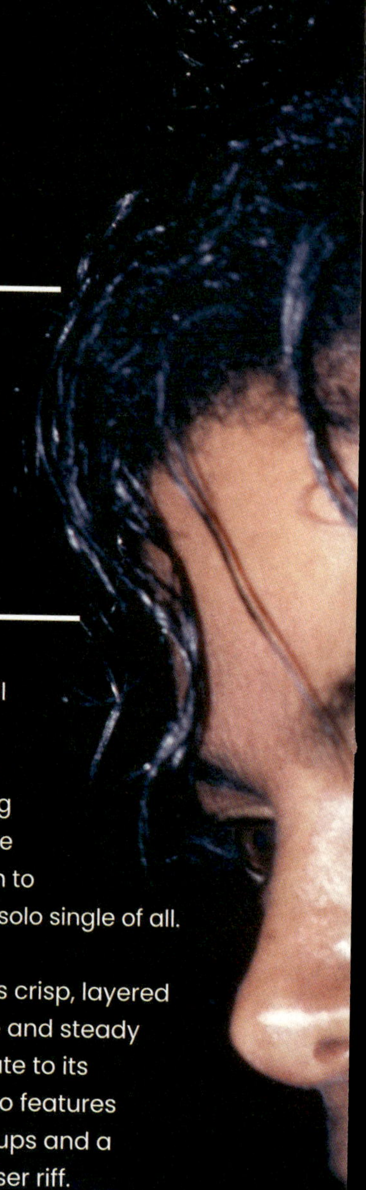

From Jackson's hit album *Thriller*, which was released on 30 November 1982, *Billie Jean* tells the story of a woman who claims that the protagonist is the father of her child. The lyrics depict the protagonist's denial and insistence that Billie Jean is lying. By exploring themes of love, deceit and the pressure of unwanted attention, Jackson reputedly drew from his own experiences with obsessive fans and the challenges of fame.

The song was a huge success, one of the best-selling singles of that year, topping the Billboard Top 100 for seven weeks, a #1 hit in the UK, Canada, France, Switzerland and Belgium, as well as reaching the Top 10 in many other countries. Its success was instrumental in *Thriller* becoming the best-selling album of all time worldwide and the song went on to became Jackson›s best-selling solo single of all.

The song is characterised by its crisp, layered production, distinctive bassline and steady drumbeat, all of which contribute to its infectious groove. The track also features Jackson's signature vocal hiccups and a memorable, haunting synthesiser riff.

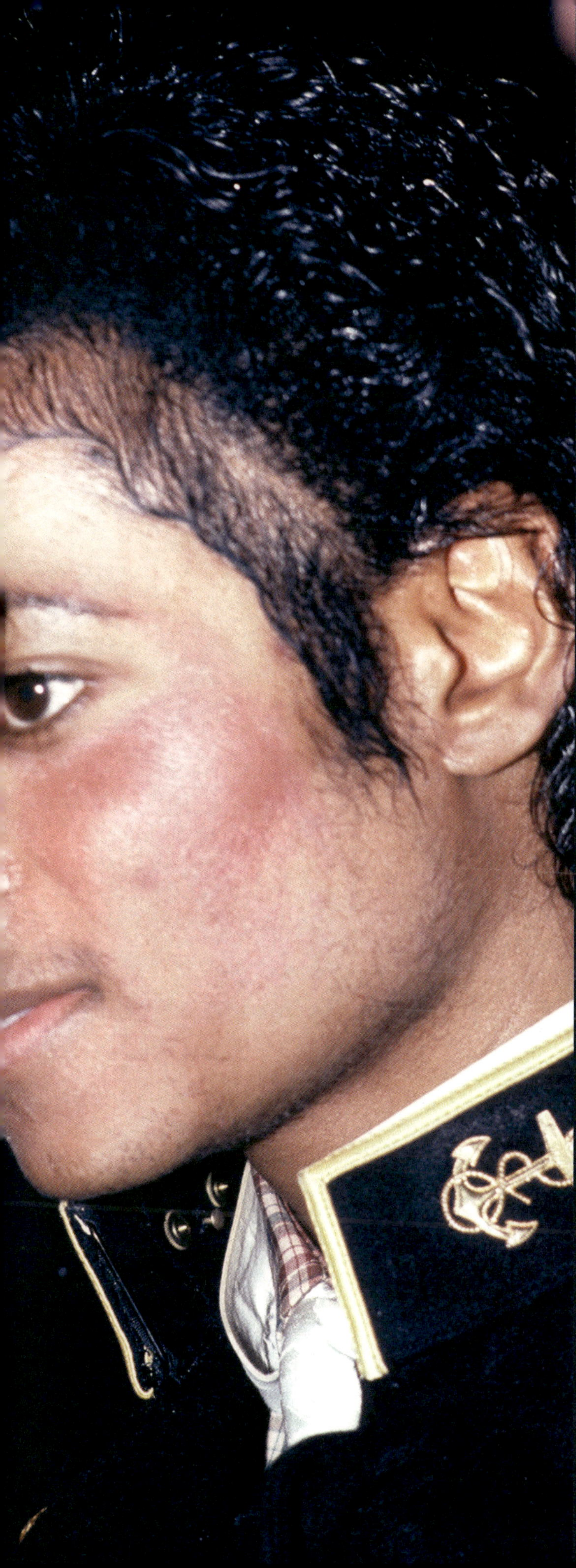

Check out these covers ...

Although it's a song which is difficult to improve, Billie Jean has been covered, sampled and referenced by countless artists. One of the best versions came from Chris Cornell, the late Soundgarden and Audioslave frontman, who performed a stripped-down, acoustic version that highlighted the song's dark and emotional undercurrents.

CHRIS CORNELL

BE MY BABY
THE RONETTES

1963

18

WRITTEN BY: Phil Spector, Ellie Greenwich and Jeff Barry

RECORDED: July 1963

PRODUCER: Phil Spector

ENGINEER: Larry Levine

RELEASED: August 1963

Released at the peak of the '60s girl group era, and including the transformative impact of Phil Spector's production techniques, *Be My Baby* captures the longing and excitement of young love in timeless fashion.

The song is renowned for showcasing Phil Spector's signature 'Wall of Sound' technique, involving a dense, layered arrangement of instruments, including drums, guitars, piano and strings, along with handclaps and castanets. This created a rich, echo-laden sound that was groundbreaking at the time. The iconic drumbeat, played by Hal Blaine, is one of the most recognisable and influential in pop music history.

Be My Baby became a massive hit, reaching #2 on the Billboard Hot 100 and #4 on the UK Singles Chart. Its success gave The Ronettes their biggest hit and helped solidify their status as one of the leading girl groups of the 1960s.

Over time the song has come to be widely regarded as one of the greatest pop tracks of all time. It has influenced countless musicians and producers, including Brian Wilson of The Beach Boys who cited it as one of his favourite records and said it had inspired some of his own work. You can't get much higher praise than that.

The song's inclusion in the opening sequence of the 1987 hit movie *Dirty Dancing* which helped introduce it to a new generation of listeners.

Check out these covers ...

Canadian singer-songwriter Andy Kim had a hit with his version in 1970, then in 1972 American singer Jody Miller's country-flavoured rendition made the country charts.

ANDY KIM

JODY MILLER

Phil Spector

BLOWIN' IN THE WIND

BOB DYLAN

1963

17

WRITTEN BY: Bob Dylan

RECORDED: 9 July 1962

PRODUCER: John H. Hammond

ENGINEER: Columbia Records studio engineer, uncredited

RELEASED: 27 May 1963

***Blowin' in the Wind* is one of the world's most famous protest songs, although its lyrics pose a series of rhetorical questions about peace, war and freedom without providing clear answers. The refrain, saying that 'the answer... is blowin' in the wind,' suggests that the solutions to these profound questions are elusive or already known, but ignored.**

The song was released on Dylan's second album, *The Freewheelin' Bob Dylan*, in 1963, before being released as a single later that year when it quickly became an anthem for the civil rights movement and anti-war protests of the era. With simple yet profound lyrics, it resonated with a generation seeking social change and justice.

The song's universal themes and poignant questions about humanity's struggles made it timeless and relevant beyond the 1960s and it remains one of Bob Dylan's most celebrated songs, symbolising the power of music to address social and political issues. Above all it stands out for its simplicity, depth and enduring relevance.

It's this ongoing relevance and recognition that underscores Dylan's influence as a storyteller extraordinaire, who revolutionised the art of songwriting by blending poetic and literary elements with music. The quality of his lyrics, which were often rich with social commentary, abstract imagery and personal introspection, pushed the boundaries of what popular music could express. This achievement was recognised in 2016 when Dylan was awarded the Nobel Prize in Literature for his contributions to songwriting, making him the first musician to receive this honour.

Check out these covers ...

Among the many artists who have recorded *Blowin' in the Wind*, American folk music trio Peter, Paul and Mary had the biggest hit when their 1963 version, issued just a few weeks after Dylan's album came out, reached #2 on the Billboard Hot 100 chart. Other covers have been released by Stevie Wonder, Sam Cooke and Joan Baez.

JOAN BAEZ

SAM COOKE

STEVIE WONDER

PETER, PAUL & MARY

SPACE ODDITY
DAVID BOWIE
1969

16

WRITTEN BY: David Bowie

RECORDED: June 1969

PRODUCER: Gus Dudgeon

ENGINEER: Ken Scott

RELEASED: 11 July 1969

Among David Bowie's most popular and significant songs, *Space Oddity* marked a major breakthrough in his career, establishing him as an important artist. Telling the story of Major Tom, an astronaut who becomes stranded in space, it explores themes of isolation, introspection and the human need for connection.

Key to its important place in Bowie's legacy is that it captured the zeitgeist of the space race era, coinciding with the Apollo 11 moon landing when US astronaut Neil Armstrong became the first human to set foot on the moon on 20 July 1969.

The song's innovative use of space-themed lyrics, atmospheric production and Bowie's haunting vocal performance chimed with the public mood at the time and made it a commercial success. It reached the top five in the UK Singles Chart upon its release and became a #1 hit when it was re-released in 1975. *Space Oddity* was included on David Bowie's second studio album, originally released under the title *David Bowie* in the UK on 4 November 1969. The album was later reissued as *Space Oddity* in 1972 by RCA Records to capitalize on the success of the single.

However, the song's impact extends beyond its initial success. It is also notable for introducing the world to Bowie's fascination with alter egos and conceptual storytelling, themes that recurred throughout his career. Major Tom would later reappear in more of Bowie's work, most notably in the 1980 song *Ashes to Ashes* where Bowie portrays Major Tom as a drug addict.

Although initially seen as a topical novelty track, its subsequent success helped establish Bowie as a pioneering artist who was unafraid to explore new themes and sounds. The majestic sonic creativity he used on this song has made it a classic.

Check out these covers ...

Space Oddity has been widely covered by a range of artists including Def Leppard and The Smashing Pumpkins. A 2013 cover by Canadian astronaut Chris Hadfield, who recorded a version of the song while he was aboard the International Space Station, went viral and brought the song to a new generation of listeners.

CHRIS HADFIELD

THE SMASHING PUMPKINS

BRIDGE OVER TROUBLED WATER

SIMON & GARFUNKEL

1970

15

WRITTEN BY: Paul Simon

RECORDED: Between November 1969 and January 1970

PRODUCER: Roy Halee, Paul Simon and Art Garfunkel

ENGINEER: Roy Halee

RELEASED: 26 January 1970

The soothing ballad *Bridge over Troubled Water* became one of the defining songs of the 1970s.

Written as an expression of unconditional love and solidarity, to offer comfort and support, the song has been associated with moments of national and personal significance ever since and is often performed at charity events, memorials and public gatherings.

Its message of hope and comfort has made it a universal anthem during times of crisis and reflection as the lyrics convey themes of reassurance and solace, as the singer promises to be a metaphorical 'bridge' over life's hardships and challenges.

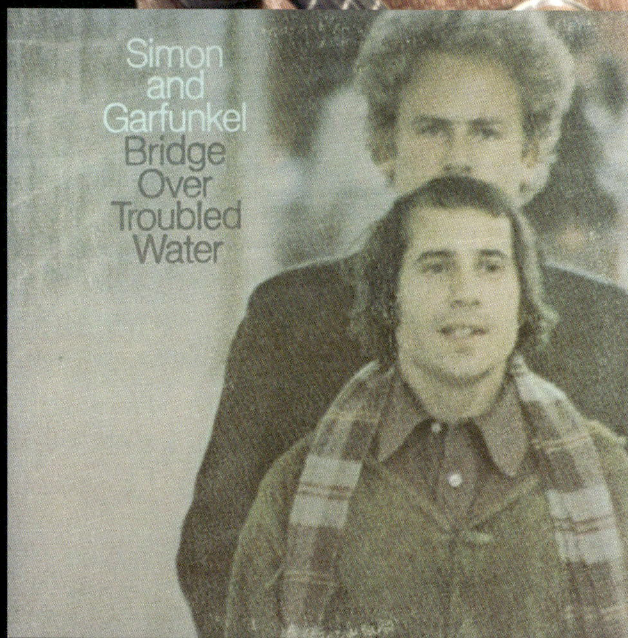

Art Garfunkel's soaring lead vocals add a profound emotional depth and sincerity to the song which, combined with a rich musical arrangement including the gentle piano accompaniment, strings and a gospel choir, creates a powerful and moving listening experience.

The song was released as a single on 26 January 1970, the same day as the duo's fifth, and as things turned out, final studio album, for which it was the title track. It topped the charts in multiple countries, including the US where it remained at #1 on the Billboard Hot 100 for six weeks. Its commercial success helped solidify Simon and Garfunkel's status as one of the leading musical acts of their time.

Critically acclaimed, *Bridge over Troubled Water* won Grammy Awards in 1971 for Record of the Year, Song of the Year, Best Contemporary Song and Best Engineered Record (Non-Classical), while the album was Album of the Year.

Check out these covers ...

As one of Simon & Garfunkel's most cherished songs, *Bridge Over Troubled Water* has inspired many artists. Aretha Franklin, Elvis Presley and LeAnn Rimes, among others, have introduced the song to new audiences and generations. Aretha Franklin's version, infused with gospel elements, is one of the most celebrated, and also widely considered to be among the best covers of all time. Released as a single in March 1971, it made #1 on the R&B singles chart and #6 on the Billboard Hot 100. Featured on her album *Aretha Live at Fillmore West,* it also won a Grammy Award for Best Female R&B Vocal Performance in 1972.

ARETHA FRANKLIN

ELVIS PRESLEY

LEANN RIMES

AMERICAN PIE
DON MCLEAN
1971

14

WRITTEN BY: Don McLean

RECORDED: Between May and June 1971

PRODUCER: Ed Freeman

ENGINEER: Tom Flye

RELEASED: October 1971

More than just a song, *American Pie* has become more of a cultural artefact capturing the spirit of an era. Ever popular, its narrative of change and loss, coupled with its memorable melody and sing-along chorus, continues to evoke reflection and discussion about the American experience.

It is a richly allegorical reflection on the changes in American society and music from the late 1950s to the early 1970s. The lyrics are a nostalgic lament for the innocence and optimism of the early rock 'n' roll era, and famously reference 'the day the music died', which alludes to the tragic plane crash on 3 February 1959, that killed Buddy Holly, Ritchie Valens and J.P. 'The Big Bopper' Richardson.

These thoughts are contrasted with the turbulent social and political changes of the 1960s that followed, using vivid imagery and numerous allusions to historical events, cultural shifts and musical milestones. While fans and critics have spent decades analysing and interpreting the lyrics, McLean has remained largely cryptic about the specifics, adding to the song's mystique and appeal.

Released as the title track of McLean's *American Pie* album in November 1971, the song was a massive commercial success, reaching #1 on the Billboard Hot 100 in the United States and charting highly in several other countries. At 8 minutes and 42 seconds long, it was the longest song ever to enter the Billboard Hot 100 at the time of release and remains the sixth longest song to feature on that chart. The single was certified gold in 1972 and later platinum.

Now widely regarded as one of the greatest American songs of all time, it has been preserved in the National Recording Registry by the Library of Congress for its cultural, historical and aesthetic significance.

Check out these covers ...

Madonna's dance-pop cover in 2000 brought the song back into the mainstream when it reached #1 in multiple countries.

Country music star Garth Brooks has performed American Pie live at several of his concerts, as has John Mayer; while back in 1973 fictional family band The Brady Bunch covered the song on their 1972 album *Meet the Brady Bunch.*

MADONNA

JOHN MAYER

BRADY BUNCH

HALLELUJAH
LEONARD COHEN
1984

13

WRITTEN BY: Leonard Cohen
RECORDED: June 1984
PRODUCER: John Lissauer
ENGINEER: Leanne Ungar
RELEASED: December 1984

***H**allelujah* **is a complex and multi-layered song that blends themes of spirituality, love and human emotion.**

Characterised by its haunting melody and simple, yet powerful, chord progression, the original arrangement is relatively minimalist, featuring Cohen's voice, piano and subtle synthesizer backgrounds. Cohen's deep, gravelly voice adds a layer of gravitas to the poetic lyrics which reference biblical stories, particularly the tales of King David and Samson and Delilah, while also exploring the themes of faith, doubt and redemption.

The song's recurring refrain of 'hallelujah', a Hebrew word meaning 'praise the Lord', is juxtaposed against verses that convey both reverence and a sense of brokenness. Cohen's lyrics blend the sacred and the secular, making the song both an exultant spiritual hymn and a deeply personal reflection on life's trials and tribulations.

Originally released on his 1984 album *Various Positions,* the Canadian singer/songwriter/poet Cohen reportedly wrote up to 80 drafts before he was content with it. After his death in November 2016, the song experienced another resurgence and even made the Billboard Hot 100 chart for the first time in its history.

Check out these covers …

One of the most covered tracks in music – with some 300 versions – the song's ongoing fame and impact has much to do with its reinterpretation by several other notable musicians and performers, particularly John Cale, Jeff Buckley, k.d. lang and Rufus Wainwright who most prominently covered it years after its initial release. These versions propelled the song to become the global colossus it is today.

Buckley's recording appeared on his 1994 album *Grace* and has more than 223 million views on YouTube. Cale's version featured in the 2001 film Shrek.

Leonard Cohen discussed the many and varied covers of *Hallelujah* in a 2009 interview with CBC Radio. He said that he found the sheer number of covers 'ironic and amusing,' especially considering that his record label had initially refused to release the song.

JEFF BUCKLEY

JOHN CALE

RUFUS WAINWRIGHT

YOUR SONG
ELTON JOHN
1970

12

WRITTEN BY: Elton John and Bernie Taupin

RECORDED: January 1970

PRODUCER: Gus Dudgeon

ENGINEER: Studio engineer (uncredited) under supervision of Gus Dudgeon

RELEASED: 26 October 1970

Widely regarded as one of Elton John and Bernie Taupin's greatest compositions, and certainly one of their first big hits, *Your Song* was the lead single released from Elton's self-titled second studio album, which was officially released in April 1971.

It was originally the B-side to *Take Me to the Pilot* but got so much airplay that it became the A-side.

Your Song's beautiful melody, heartfelt lyrics and Elton's emotive vocal performance, showcased his exceptional talent as a singer-songwriter, helped propel him to international stardom and laid the foundation for his astonishingly successful and long-lasting career.

The song was a huge commercial success, reaching the Top 10 in both the UK and the US. Yet its importance extends beyond its chart performance and critical acclaim. As one of Elton John's signature songs, it is a timeless classic, enduring for over five decades and inspiring countless artists across generations.

Check out these covers ...

Your Song was technically 'covered' before it was released – as an up and coming artist, Elton had been opening for the American band Three Dog Night and allowed the band to record Your Song for their album *It Ain't Easy* just before he released it himself.

Numerous artists have put their spin on the song since then, including Lady Gaga and Ellie Goulding. In film it has been sung by actor Ewan McGregor and opera singer Alessandro Safina in the 2001 hit movie *Moulin Rouge*, while Taron Egerton, playing Elton, sang it in the 2019 Elton biopic *Rocketman*.

THREE DOG NIGHT

LADY GAGA

ELLIE GOULDING

GOD ONLY KNOWS
THE BEACH BOYS

1966

11

WRITTEN BY: Brian Wilson and Tony Asher

RECORDED: Several sessions between 10 March and 11 April 1966

PRODUCER: Brian Wilson

ENGINEER: Chuck Britz

RELEASED: 18 July 1966

The Beach Boys were at the peak of their powers when they released this masterpiece, celebrated for its innovative sound, intricate arrangement, lush harmonies and emotional resonance. In the US it was the B-side to *'Wouldn't It Be Nice'*, though it became the A-side in the UK and other countries later in the year. Both songs were from their 11th album, *Pet Sounds*, now considered to be among the greatest and most influential albums in music history.

One of the most remarkable aspects of *God Only Knows* is its revolutionary approach to production. Brian Wilson,

the creative force behind The Beach Boys, pushed the boundaries of studio recording techniques, employing innovative methods such as double-tracking vocals, and incorporating unconventional instruments like French horns and accordions to achieve the dramatic baroque sound he wanted. This attention to detail and sonic experimentation resulted in a rich, layered sound that captivated audiences then and now.

The vocal performance on *God Only Knows* is nothing short of sublime, with Carl Wilson's lead vocals, exuding warmth and sincerity, widely considered to be his best ever. His bandmates' intricate backing harmonies come in to create a sonic tapestry with an enchanting ethereal quality which, coupled with lyrics about unconditional love and devotion, elevates the song to classic status.

Surprisingly, the song didn't enjoy much chart success as a single, unlike many of their other huge hits. Despite its critical acclaim and enduring popularity, it made no impression on the Billboard Hot 100 in the United States when it was initially released. However, it has had a lasting impact and it is now recognised as one of the greatest songs of all time by fellow musicians, music historians and critics alike.

With its influence still heard in countless contemporary artists who have been inspired by its melodic beauty and emotional depth, the song stands as a crown jewel in The Beach Boys' majestic musical legacy.

Check out these covers ...

To be covered by David Bowie, Paul McCartney and Elvis (Costello) is proof positive of a great track.

Bowie including *God Only Knows* in many of his live performances, as well as recording a studio version for his 1984 album *Tonight.* Next came Elvis Costello who covered the song with the Brodsky Quartet.

Then Paul McCartney, who once listed the song as one of the 'greatest ever', performed *God Only Knows* as a tribute to Brian Wilson at the Kennedy Center Honors in 2007.

Other artists who have paid tribute to the track with their own renditions include Joss Stone and The Flaming Lips.

PAUL MCCARTNEY

DAVID BOWIE

THE FLAMING LIPS

CALIFORNIA DREAMIN
THE MAMAS & THE PAPAS
1965

10

WRITTEN BY: John Phillips and Michelle Phillips

RECORDED: Winter 1965

PRODUCER: Lou Adler

ENGINEER: Bones Howe

RELEASED: December 1965

With its distinctive blend of folk-rock and pop sensibilities, *California Dreamin'* features lush vocal harmonies, evocative lyrics and a catchy melody which combined to create a timeless anthem of the 1960s.

Husband and wife songwriting team and band members John and Michelle Phillips captured the spirit of longing, nostalgia and wanderlust that defined the era when the song was released in 1965 as a single, and later included on the group's debut album, *If You Can Believe Your Eyes and Ears.*

Upon its release, *California Dreamin'* quickly climbed the charts, peaking at #4 on the Billboard Hot 100 chart in the United States and reaching the top 10 in Canada and the UK, among others.

One of the key factors contributing to the song's impact was its relatable themes and universal appeal as it spoke to a generation of young people yearning for escape and adventure.

The Mamas & the Papas' impeccable vocal performances further elevated the song, with lead vocals by Denny Doherty and Cass Elliot complemented by the harmonies of John Phillips and Michelle Phillips. Their seamless blend of voices created a sound that was rich, soulful and utterly captivating, drawing listeners in with each soaring chorus and haunting refrain.

Check out these covers ...

Beyond its chart success and critical acclaim, *California Dreamin'* has left a lasting impact on popular culture, influencing countless artists and musicians over the decades since its release. The iconic opening riff and memorable lyrics have been sampled, referenced and covered by artists across a wide range of genres, including Diana Krall, Bobby Womack, Sia, The Beach Boys and Queen Latifah.

DIANA KRALL

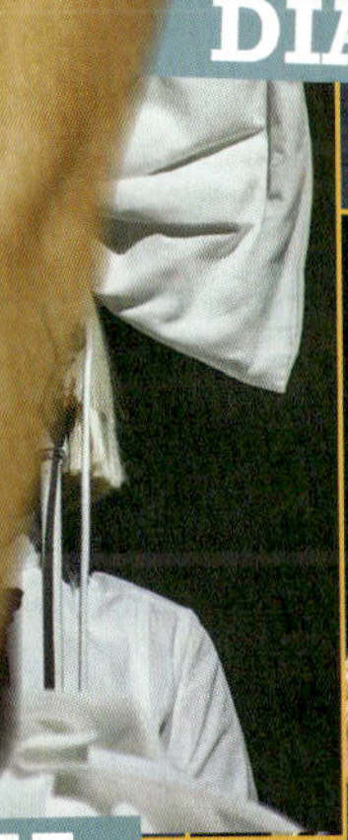

IA

BOBBY WOMACK

SUPERSTITION
STEVIE WONDER
1972

9

WRITTEN BY: Stevie Wonder

RECORDED: May – July 1972

PRODUCER: Stevie Wonder, Robert Margouleff and Malcolm Cecil

ENGINEER: Austin Godsey and Joan DeCola

RELEASED: 24 October 1972

Originally known as Little Stevie Wonder, a teenage prodigy who signalled his extraordinary talent by first conquering the US charts at the age of 13 with *Fingertips,* Stevie grew up to establish himself as the preeminent genius of Motown during the 1970s.

Among his string of groundbreaking albums, 1972's *Talking Book* spawned the hit song *Superstition* – a masterclass in funk and soul, blending compelling grooves, powerful vocals and a memorable melody to create a timeless classic.

At the heart of *Superstition* is its irresistible percussive rhythm, driven by a funky clavinet riff that instantly grabs the attention. Stevie Wonder's virtuosic performance on the clavinet, attacking the keys like he had a funky guitar, combined with the dynamic interplay of bass, drums and horns to create a sound that is both irresistibly danceable and musically sophisticated.

Lyrically, *Superstition* explores the impact of superstition on human behaviour and caution against the dangers of relying on it to guide one's actions, urging listeners to think for themselves instead and break free from irrational beliefs.

The song was massively successful, reaching #1 on the Billboard Hot 100 chart in America and making #11 in the UK. It earned the artist the first of his Grammy awards – for 'Best Rhythm & Blues Song' and 'Best R&B Vocal Performance, Male' in 1974.

Now one of the most celebrated artists in Grammy history, Stevie is in the record books as a visionary artist who has inspired generations with his soulful voice and innovative compositions.

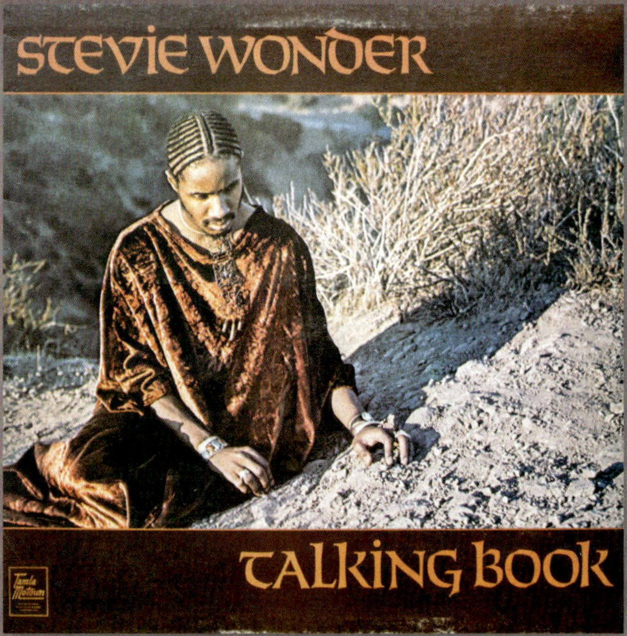

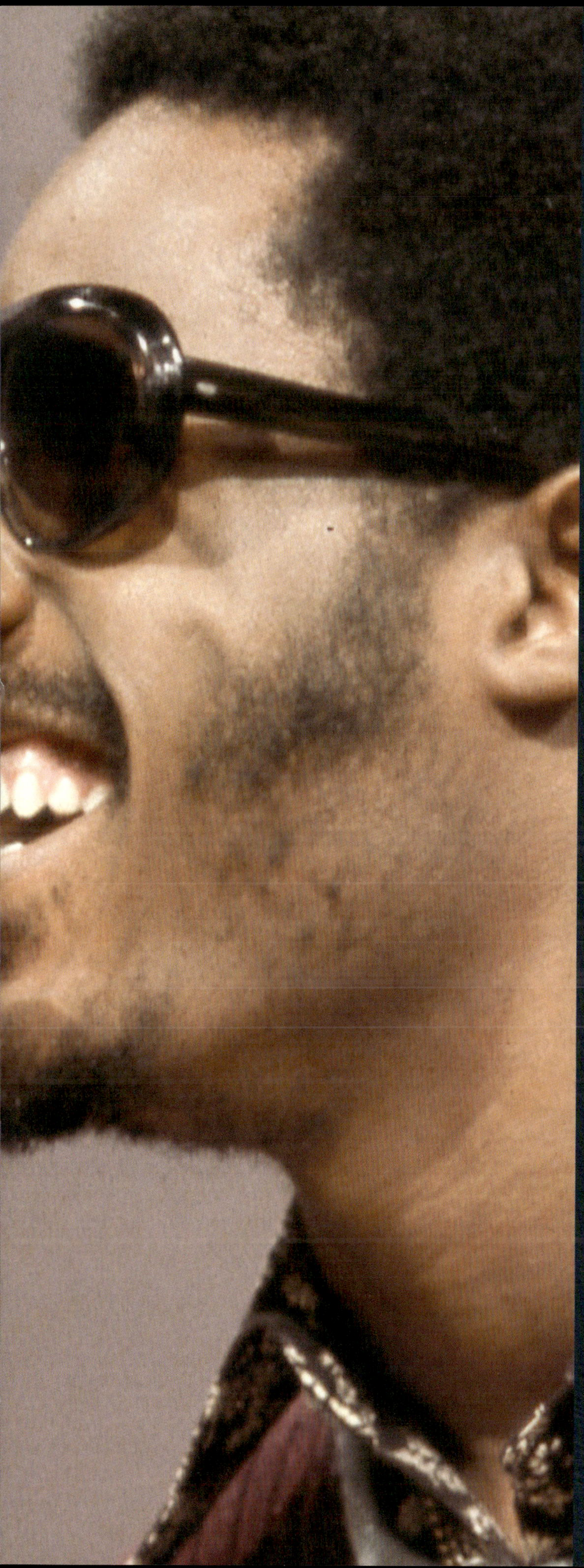

Check out these covers ...

Popular with numerous artists across different genres, *Superstition* has most memorably been covered by renowned blues guitarist Stevie Ray Vaughan, guitar virtuoso Jeff Beck, who included a cover on his 1973 album *Beck, Bogert & Appice,* and the Red Hot Chili Peppers who have incorporated *Superstition* into their live performances on numerous occasions.

Queen Bey – Beyoncé herself – famously performed *Superstition* during her halftime show at the Super Bowl in 2013. Her electrifying performance, complete with elaborate choreography and powerful vocals, captivated millions of viewers and solidified the song's status as a timeless classic.

RED HOT CHILI PEPPERS

BEYONCÉ

DANCING IN THE STREET
MARTHA AND THE VANDELLAS
1964

8

WRITTEN BY: Marvin Gaye, William "Mickey" Stevenson and Ivy Jo Hunter
RECORDED: Spring 1964
PRODUCER: William "Mickey" Stevenson and Ivy Jo Hunter
ENGINEER: Uncredited studio engineer
RELEASED: July 1964

Originally conceived as a love song, *Dancing in the Street* evolved into something far bigger. Led by the dynamic Martha Reeves, the girl group Martha and the Vandellas infused the song with a sense of urgency and exuberance, turning it into a rallying cry for social change and cultural revolution.

Its call to action invited people of all backgrounds to come together and celebrate their common humanity through the universal language of music and dance. The song's lyrics speak of city streets coming alive with the sounds of music, as people from every walk of life join in the revelry, transcending barriers of race, class and nationality.

While most celebrated for its joyous and celebratory vibe, the song also took on political connotations during the civil rights movement when some interpreted the lyrics and the imagery of people dancing in the streets as a call for social change and a symbol of African American empowerment.

As well as reaching #1 on the US Billboard Hot R&B Singles chart, #2 on the Billboard Hot 100 chart in the United States and #4 in the UK in 1964, *Dancing in the Street* also holds a special place in the history of the legendary Motown Records. As one of the label's signature hits, the song showcased Motown's trademark blend of soul, rhythm and blues, and pop sensibility, earning Martha and the Vandellas widespread acclaim and recognition.

Martha's electrifying vocals were reportedly given extra oomph because she stood on her tiptoes to reach the microphone, adding an extra layer of energy and intensity to her delivery. The handclaps heard throughout the song were not planned in advance

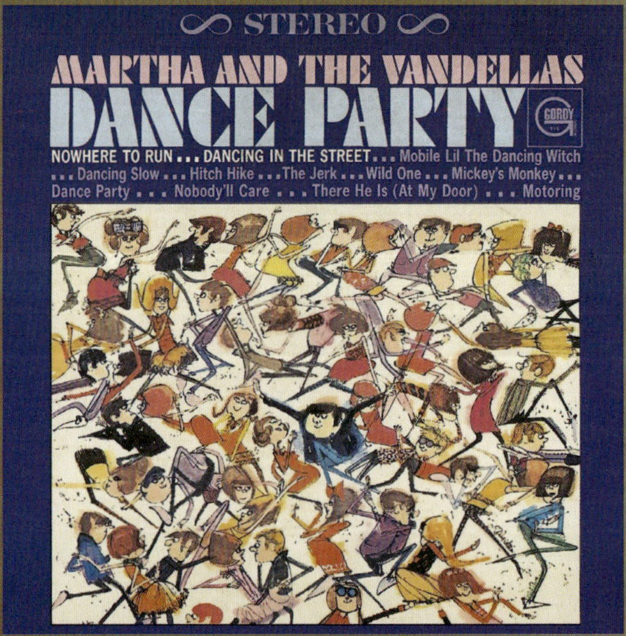

but were instead a spontaneous addition during the recording session as Martha and the Vandellas and other studio musicians joined in, clapping along to the rhythm, adding to the song's infectious energy.

Check out these covers ...

A large and diverse group of artists have covered *Dancing In The Streets,* including The Mamas & The Papas, The Kinks and even The Grateful Dead. But most memorably legendary rock stars David Bowie and Mick Jagger made the song their own in an iconic and energetic duet for the Live Aid charity in 1985. The recording was supported by memorable video which is one of the most talked-about of all time. The two stars were filmed overnight dancing and prancing around London's emerging docklands area for a highly camp film which was shown on the screens of both the New York and the London stadiums during the mammoth Live Aid benefit gig.

Advert for David Bowie and Mick Jagger's version

I WANT TO HOLD YOUR HAND
THE BEATLES
1963

7

WRITTEN BY: John Lennon/Paul McCartney
RECORDED: 17 October 1963
PRODUCER: George Martin
ENGINEER: Norman Smith
RELEASED: 29 Nov 1963 (UK); 26 Dec 1963 (US)

This quintessential '60s pop song from The Beatles topped the charts on both sides of the Atlantic. It provided the band with their third British #1 and their first hit in America where it remained at #1 on the Billboard Hot 100 chart for seven consecutive weeks from 1 February 1964.

With an irresistible melody and infectious energy, this iconic track ignited the frenzy of Beatlemania which would accompany the band during the early years of their career and kickstarted the 'British Invasion' of the American charts.

John Lennon and Paul McCartney, the prolific songwriting duo behind The Beatles' most beloved tunes, collaborated on the song, which was the first Beatles record to be made using four-track recording equipment. The Beatles also recorded a version of the song for the German market, as *'Komm, Gib Mir Deine Hand'* which gave them another #1.

In the UK the song stayed at #1 for five weeks after entering the charts on 14 December 1963, knocking the Beatles previous hit *She Loves You* off the top spot in the first example of an act taking over from itself at the top of the chart.

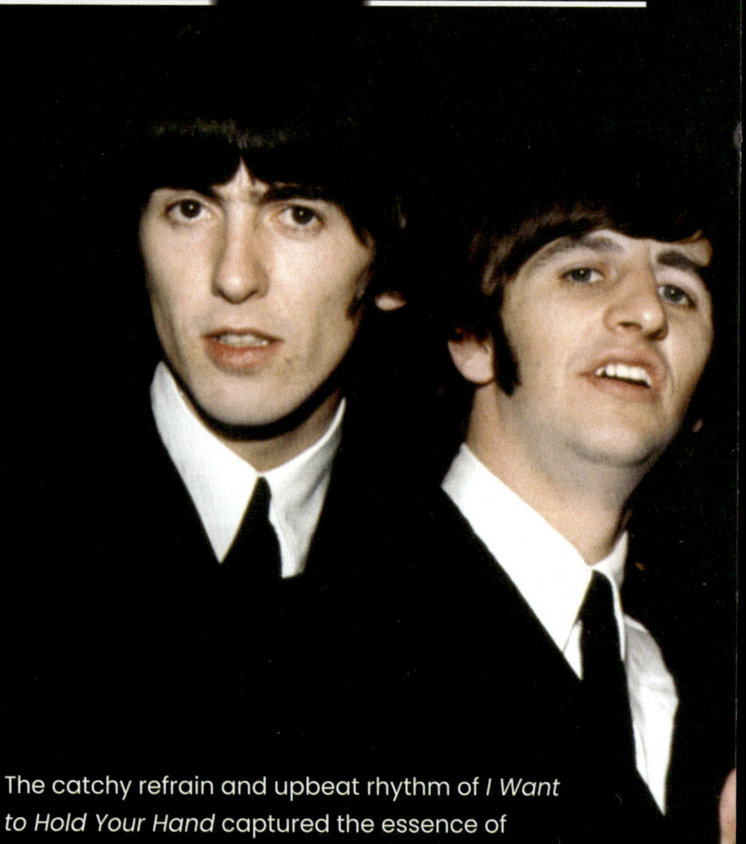

The catchy refrain and upbeat rhythm of *I Want to Hold Your Hand* captured the essence of the optimistic 1960s, catapulting The Beatles to superstardom and leaving an indelible mark on popular music history. Its enduring popularity and cultural significance continues to be felt decades after its release, solidifying its status as among the very greatest songs of all time.

Promo for I Want to Hold Your Hand

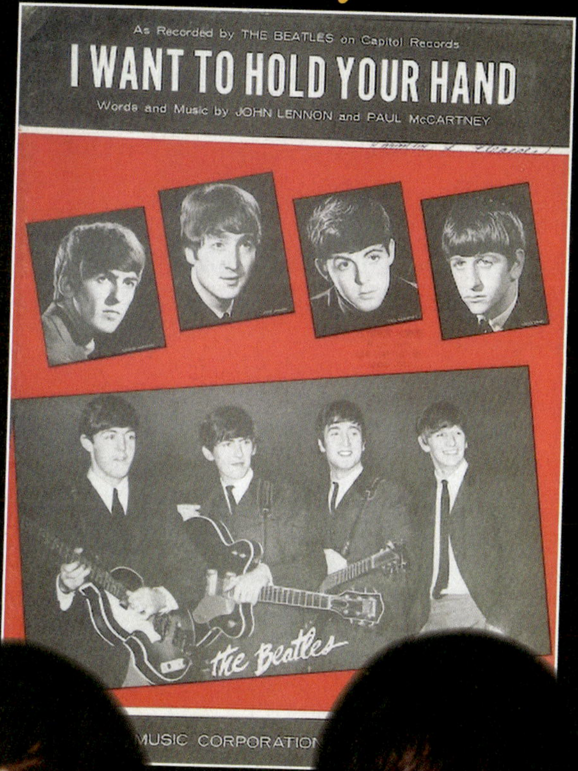

Check out these covers ...

The Soul legend Al Green recorded a soulful rendition of "I Wanna Hold Your Hand" in 1969, infusing his signature style into the song. Then Dollar, the popular 80s duo also covered the track, reaching #9 in the British charts.

DOLLAR

AL GREEN

German Version

BOHEMIAN RHAPSODY

QUEEN

1975

6

WRITTEN BY: Freddie Mercury

RECORDED: August 1975

PRODUCER: Queen and Roy Thomas Baker

ENGINEER: Mike Stone

RELEASED: 31 October 1975

The mammoth masterpiece *Bohemian Rhapsody* by legendary British rock band Queen reigns supreme as one of the most iconic songs in the history of popular music.

Released in 1975 as part of their album *A Night at the Opera*, the song defied conventional songwriting norms with its innovative structure, genre-bending sound and epic scale. It was a six-minute long showcase for the band's immense talent and creative vision.

It is more than just a song – it's a musical journey that traverses multiple sections, from haunting balladry to operatic grandeur to hard rock intensity in a complex arrangement. Its seamless integration of disparate musical styles set it apart from anything else in the contemporary music landscape, earning it immediate attention and acclaim.

One of the most striking aspects of Bohemian Rhapsody are the enigmatic lyrics, open to interpretation, but covering themes of existentialism, betrayal and redemption.

The band's magnetic frontman and singer Freddie Mercury added emotional depth and intensity to the sound with his powerful vocal delivery, ranging from delicate falsettos to thunderous wails. It all combined to make Bohemian Rhapsody a massive success. The song made the top of the charts in multiple countries, including the UK, where it spent nine weeks at #1 and also the US where it peaked at #9.

Breaking new ground in studio production techniques and pushing the boundaries of what was possible in a recording studio, the song's success paved the way for other ambitious and experimental works in rock music, inspiring generations of artists to explore the possibilities of creativity and innovation.

Check out these covers ...

An eclectic list of artists have reinterpreted Bohemian Rhapsody including:

- Panic! At The Disco who covered the song for the soundtrack of the 2016 film *Suicide Squad*, paying homage to the original while adding a unique flair and energy of their own.
- The Muppets performed a humorous rendition of Bohemian Rhapsody in a music video released in 2009. The video features various Muppet characters singing and performing the song in their own comedic style.
- British singer-songwriter Elton John gave a powerful rendition of *Bohemian Rhapsody* during his *One Night Only* concert at Madison Square Garden in 2000, showcasing his own vocal range and showmanship.
- American singer-songwriter Pink covered the song in a rock-infused style during her 2009 'Funhouse Tour'.

PANIC! AT THE DISCO

PINK

LOLA
THE KINKS
1970

5

WRITTEN BY: Ray Davies
RECORDED: April 1970
PRODUCER: Ray Davies
ENGINEER: Mike Bocak
RELEASED: June 1970

The Kinks, and their brilliant frontman and songwriter Ray Davies, were in need of renewed commercial success when the groundbreaking *Lola* sashayed up the charts in 1970. Having enjoyed huge record sales and acclaim in the 1960s and become part of the British Invasion of the US charts, the band's progress across the Atlantic stalled when they fell foul of the American unions and were banned from touring there. They then went three years without a Top Ten record in the UK before *Lola* – from the album *Lola Versus Powerman and the Moneygoround, Part One* – restored their fortunes, becoming became a huge transatlantic hit.

Its raw energy, acoustic guitar sound and distinctive riff, played by Ray's brother Dave Davies, may well have been enough to break their dry patch anyway, but what made the song such a standout were the lyrics which told the story of a young man meeting a transgender woman named Lola in a club. This unconventional narrative, based on the real life experience of one of Ray's friends, sparked intrigue and discussion, making it the first major hit with an explicit LGBTQ theme years ahead of its time.

Interestingly, the controversial content around sexual ambiguity largely evaded the scrutiny of BBC censors, who only objected to the mention of Coca-Cola in the lyrics due to their policy against commercial references. In response, Ray Davies provided an alternate version writing and splicing in the phrase 'cherry cola' in place of the brand name.

Despite coming up with the song's famous riff, Ray's brother Dave didn't get a credit for the song which exacerbated the already simmering tension between the siblings, which went on for years and eventually erupted in the band's demise in 1996.

Check out these covers ...

English post-punk band *The Raincoats* covered *Lola* on their self-titled debut album released in 1979, offering a unique interpretation of the song with an alternative rock style. During the 1990s British rock band Blur often performed a playful and energetic live cover of *Lola* at their concerts.

THE RAINCOATS

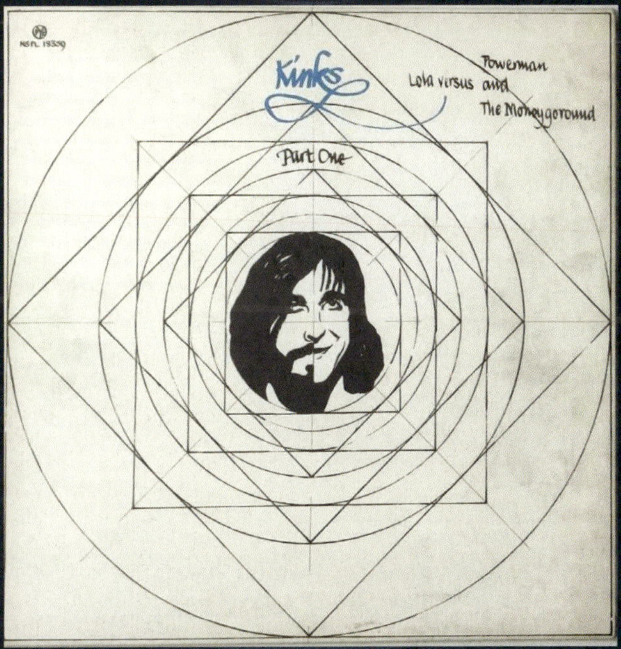

CAN'T HELP FALLING IN LOVE

ELVIS PRESLEY

1961

4

WRITTEN BY: Hugo Peretti, Luigi Creatore and George David Weiss

RECORDED: March 1961

PRODUCER: Steve Sholes

ENGINEER: Bill Porter

RELEASED: 21 November 1961

C*an't Help Falling in Love* is one of Elvis Presley's signature songs and his greatest love ballad. Released in 1961 as part of the soundtrack for his film *Blue Hawaii,* it quickly became a classic and remains a fan favourite.

The *Blue Hawaii* soundtrack stayed at #1 in the US charts for 20 consecutive weeks in the autumn of 1961, while the single reached #1 and #2 in the UK and US charts respectively.

Using his velvety vocals to exude a sense of tender vulnerability, Elvis is singing about the inevitability of falling deeply in love. The song's sentimental lyrics are perfectly complemented by gentle instrumentation, featuring lush strings and a subtle rhythm.

With its universal theme of love and devotion capturing the very essence of romance, the song has become a standard with enduring appeal and is a popular choice at weddings for the 'first dance'.

Elvis frequently sang it as a concert finale and so it became the last song he performed live, at his concert in Indianapolis on 26 June 1977, just before his death on 16 August that year.

German movie poster for Blue Hawaii

Check out these covers ...

Beyond its commercial success, *Can't Help Falling in Love* holds a special place in popular culture and has been covered by numerous artists.

Its most successful reinterpretation came in 1993 when British reggae band UB40 reached #1 on both sides of the Atlantic with their cover.

American singer Haley Reinhart who found fame on American Idol, went viral with her version which was used in a commercial for Extra Gum, and was eventually certified platinum in 2023.

UB40

HALEY REINHART

LIFE ON MARS?
DAVID BOWIE
1973

3

WRITTEN BY: David Bowie

RECORDED: 1971

PRODUCER: David Bowie and Ken Scott

ENGINEER: Ken Scott

RELEASED: 22 June 1973 (single re-release)

L*ife on Mars?* stands as one of David Bowie's most revered and enduring compositions. With its great melody, sublime chord progression and sweeping strings the stylistically adventurous song encapsulates Bowie's boundless creativity and distinctive musical style. First heard in 1971 as a track on his album *Hunky Dory*, the song has gone on to resonate with audiences for the many decades since as one of the most stylistically adventurous compositions of all time.

From its haunting piano introduction to Bowie's emotive vocal delivery, *Life on Mars?* is a masterclass in storytelling through music. The song's enigmatic lyrics weave a surreal narrative tackling themes of disillusionment, escapism and existential questioning. Its evocative imagery invites listeners into a world of vivid imagination and introspection, making it a timeless piece of artistry.

Chart-wise, *Life on Mars?* was a slow burner which didn't achieve immediate commercial success. In fact its initially reception might best be described as lukewarm. Rereleased in 1973 to capitalise on Bowie's fame with stage persona Ziggy Stardust, it peaked at a relatively modest # 3 in the UK Singles Chart. However, its impact goes far beyond chart positions as its influence has grown steadily over the years, solidifying its status as a timeless classic in Bowie's extensive repertoire.

Offering a poignant reflection on the human experience, *Life on Mars?* has been included in various films, television shows and commercials, cementing its status as a cultural touchstone.

Check out these covers …

Although it's not Bowie's most covered composition (that honour goes to *Heroes* and *Rebel Rebel*) many artists have put their own spin on Life on Mars? Among the most popular:

- Barbra Streisand was the first international star to cover the track, on her 1974 album *ButterFly*, using her powerful vocals and orchestral arrangement to reinterpret the song.
- Brazilian musician Seu Jorge recorded an acoustic Portuguese-language cover for the soundtrack of the 2004 film *The Life Aquatic with Steve Zissou*, which even earned praise from Bowie himself.
- Then Norwegian singer-songwriter AURORA performed a hauntingly beautiful rendition of *Life on Mars?* for the HBO series *Girls*, adding ethereal vocals and an atmospheric production to the song.

YESTERDAY
THE BEATLES

1966

2

WRITTEN BY: Lennon and McCartney

RECORDED: 14 June 1965

PRODUCER: George Martin

ENGINEER: Norman Smith

RELEASED: 4 March 1966

Although credited as a Lennon and McCartney composition on The Beatles album *Help*, the song *Yesterday* was primarily written by Paul McCartney. Although he and John Lennon had collaborated on writing The Beatles' early songs, by 1965, most of their compositions were predominantly the work of either one of them. However, they maintained the practice of crediting all their songs as Lennon/McCartney.

Paul has said that the melody came to him in a dream, and as soon as he woke up, he recorded it on a nearby piano to ensure he remembered it. Initially, he wondered if he had subconsciously borrowed the melody from another song, but after verifying its originality, he developed the lyrics to accompany the melody. For some time the phrase 'scrambled eggs' was used as a placeholder to fit the three syllables needed, before he came up with 'Yesterday' and developed some melancholy lyrics around lost love and regret.

The track represented a departure from The Beatles' typical rock sound and fans appreciated its simplicity, beauty and emotional depth.

Paul's heartfelt vocal performance was also hugely praised, along with the song's memorable melody.

The addition of a string quartet lent the song a classical elegance and the overall arrangement further elevated the emotional impact of the song. It did however mean that the song was the first that could not be sung live by just the Fab Four themselves. So it was performed by Paul alone, accompanying himself on acoustic guitar, marking the move towards each Beatle doing more independent work.

Check out these covers ...

Yesterday is the most covered pop song of all time, and among the most recorded of all genres. Among the many hundreds of artists to have put their own spin on the song are such greats as Elvis Presley, Frank Sinatra, Ray Charles, Marvin Gaye and Willie Nelson.

FRANK SINATRA

MARVIN GAYE

WILLIE NELSON

RAY CHARLES

IMAGINE
JOHN LENNON
1971

1

WRITTEN BY: John Lennon – Yoko Ono

RECORDED: Between 27 May and 4 July 1971

PRODUCER: Yoko Ono and Phil Spector

ENGINEER: Roy Cicala

RELEASED: 8 Oct 1971 (UK) 9 Sep 1971 (US)

***Imagine*, one of John Lennon's most celebrated and enduring songs, also featured as the title track of his album of the same name. The song's release came during a tumultuous period in Lennon's life, following the breakup of The Beatles and his ongoing activism for peace and social justice. Its incredible impact cemented Lennon's position as one of the all-time greatest songwriters of the 20th century in his own right, rather than in partnership with Paul McCartney.**

Immediately capturing the public's imagination with its powerful message of hope, peace and unity, its simple yet profound lyrics, accompanied by Lennon's hauntingly beautiful melody, resonated deeply with audiences around the world. Lennon later said he had been inspired by poems from his wife Yoko Ono's 1964 book *Grapefruit* and in June 2017 Yoko was finally officially credited as co-writer of the song by the National Music Publishers' Association in America.

One of Lennon's highest charting solo singles, the song has received widespread critical acclaim and commercial success. In the US it peaked at #3 on the Billboard Hot 100 chart, and in the UK it reached #6 on the UK Singles Chart. The single re-entered the UK charts after Lennon's murder on 8 December 1980, staying at #1 for four weeks.

It remains one of Lennon's best-selling and most beloved works, certified platinum for million-plus sales multiple times around the world.

Beyond its chart performance, *Imagine* has become an anthem for peace and a cultural touchstone. Its message of imagining a world without borders, divisions, or conflicts continues to strike a chord with listeners, transcending musical genres and generations.

John and Yoko's "Bed-in" protest

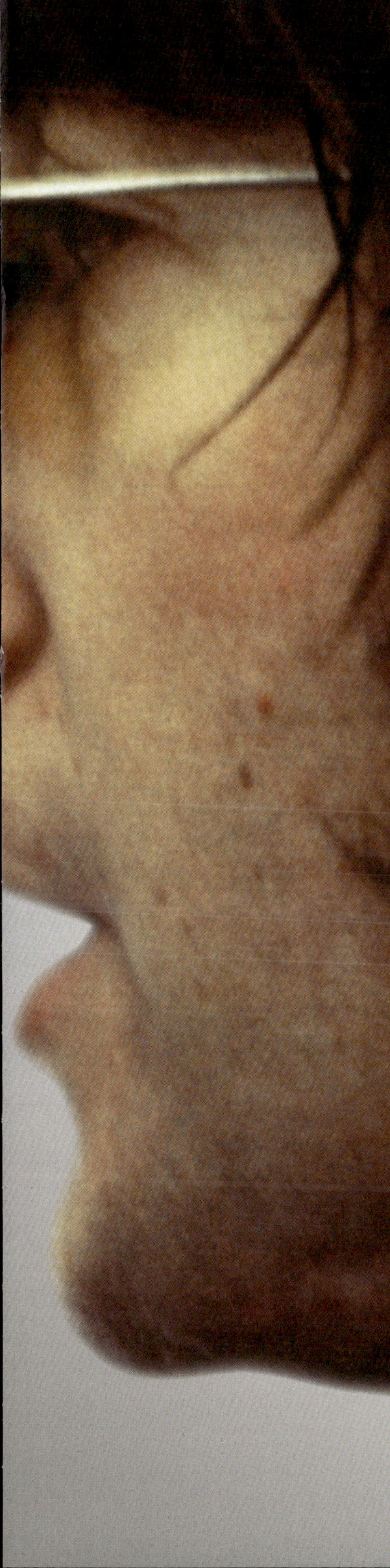

Check out these covers ...

Numerous artists have recorded *Imagine* including Joan Baez, Diana Ross, Eva Cassidy, and Dolly Parton, while other musical greats, including Elton John, David Bowie and Queen have performed the song on various occasions commemorating Lennon. In a tradition dating back to 1986, *Imagine* is performed every New Year's Eve in New York City, just before the countdown to midnight.

DIANA ROSS

EVA CASSIDY

JOAN BAEZ

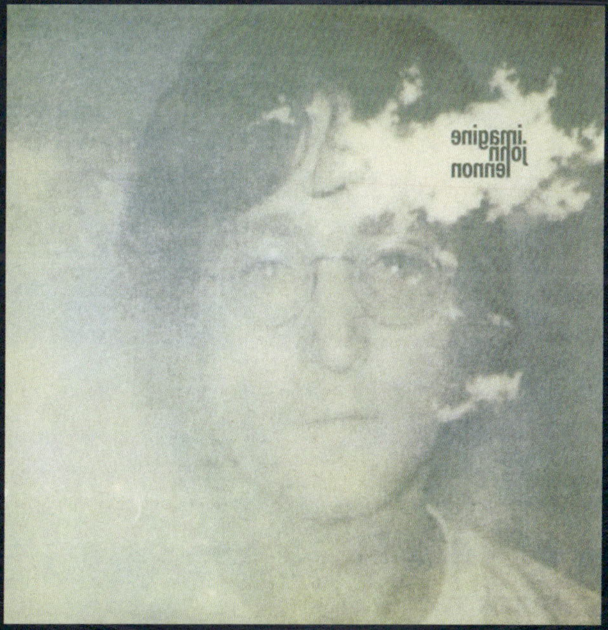

PICTURE CREDITS

Photography courtesy of

Getty images:

Dave Hogan
Michael Ochs Archives
Cyrus Andrews/Michael Ochs Archives
Fin Costello/Redferns
David Redfern/Redferns
GAB Archive/Redferns
Gems/Redferns
Kevin Mazur/MPL/WireImage for MPL
Paul Natkin/WireImage
Kevin Winter
Tim Roney
Michael Putland
King Collection/Avalon
Martyn Goodacre
Mark and Colleen Hayward/Redferns
Chris Carroll/Corbis
Koh Hasebe/Shinko Music
FG/Bauer-Griffin
Siegfried Pilz/United Archives
James Fry
Paramount Pictures
Hulton Archive
Robin Platzer
Fotos International
Walter Iooss Jr.
Jason Squires/WireImage
RB/Redferns
David Warner Ellis/Redferns
Gai Terrell/Redferns
Jim McCrary/Redferns
Mick Hutson/Redferns
Estate Of Keith Morris/Redferns
Lex van Rossen/MAI/Redferns
Richard E. Aaron/Redferns
Paul Bergen/Redferns
Gijsbert Hanekroot/Redferns
Tom Hill/WireImage
TPLP
Aaron Rapoport/Corbis Outline
Gilles Petard/Redferns
Thierry Orban/Sygma
Eileen Polk
Gie Knaeps
Silver Screen Collection
Raphael Gaillarde/Gamma-Rapho
Ross Marino
Rick Diamond
Soul Train
Jacques Pavlovsky/Sygma/Corbis
Steve Rapport

Alamy images:

Records
Rajko Simunovic
Photo 12
United Archives GmbH
Vinyls
AJ Pics
David Lichtneker
Pictorial Press Ltd
Imusic
Newscom
Allstar Picture Library Limited
CBW
Everett Collection, Inc.
sjvinyl
Entertainment Pictures
Collection Christophel
Sam Oaksey
BFA
Gijsbert Hanekroot

Other images Wiki Commons